C-4988

CAREER EXAMINATION SERIE

MW00817224

THIS IS YOUR **PASSBOOK**® FOR ...

BULK MAIL TECHNICIAN (USPS)

NLC®

NATIONAL LEARNING CORPORATION®

passbooks.com

COPYRIGHT NOTICE

This book is SOLELY intended for, is sold ONLY to, and its use is RESTRICTED to individual, bona fide applicants or candidates who qualify by virtue of having seriously filed applications for appropriate license, certificate, professional and/or promotional advancement, higher school matriculation, scholarship, or other legitimate requirements of educational and/or governmental authorities.

This book is NOT intended for use, class instruction, tutoring, training, duplication, copying, reprinting, excerption, or adaptation, etc., by:

1) Other publishers
2) Proprietors and/or Instructors of «Coaching» and/or Preparatory Courses
3) Personnel and/or Training Divisions of commercial, industrial, and governmental organizations
4) Schools, colleges, or universities and/or their departments and staffs, including teachers and other personnel
5) Testing Agencies or Bureaus
6) Study groups which seek by the purchase of a single volume to copy and/or duplicate and/or adapt this material for use by the group as a whole without having purchased individual volumes for each of the members of the group
7) Et al.

Such persons would be in violation of appropriate Federal and State statutes.

PROVISION OF LICENSING AGREEMENTS. — Recognized educational, commercial, industrial, and governmental institutions and organizations, and others legitimately engaged in educational pursuits, including training, testing, and measurement activities, may address request for a licensing agreement to the copyright owners, who will determine whether, and under what conditions, including fees and charges, the materials in this book may be used them. In other words, a licensing facility exists for the legitimate use of the material in this book on other than an individual basis. However, it is asseverated and affirmed here that the material in this book CANNOT be used without the receipt of the express permission of such a licensing agreement from the Publishers. Inquiries re licensing should be addressed to the company, attention rights and permissions department.

All rights reserved, including the right of reproduction in whole or in part, in any form or by any means, electronic or mechanical, including photocopying, recording, or by any information storage and retrieval system, without permission in writing from the Publisher.

Copyright © 2021 by

National Learning Corporation

212 Michael Drive, Syosset, NY 11791
(516) 921-8888 • www.passbooks.com
E-mail: info@passbooks.com

PUBLISHED IN THE UNITED STATES OF AMERICA

PASSBOOK® SERIES

THE *PASSBOOK® SERIES* has been created to prepare applicants and candidates for the ultimate academic battlefield – the examination room.

At some time in our lives, each and every one of us may be required to take an examination – for validation, matriculation, admission, qualification, registration, certification, or licensure.

Based on the assumption that every applicant or candidate has met the basic formal educational standards, has taken the required number of courses, and read the necessary texts, the *PASSBOOK® SERIES* furnishes the one special preparation which may assure passing with confidence, instead of failing with insecurity. Examination questions – together with answers – are furnished as the basic vehicle for study so that the mysteries of the examination and its compounding difficulties may be eliminated or diminished by a sure method.

This book is meant to help you pass your examination provided that you qualify and are serious in your objective.

The entire field is reviewed through the huge store of content information which is succinctly presented through a provocative and challenging approach – the question-and-answer method.

A climate of success is established by furnishing the correct answers at the end of each test.

You soon learn to recognize types of questions, forms of questions, and patterns of questioning. You may even begin to anticipate expected outcomes.

You perceive that many questions are repeated or adapted so that you can gain acute insights, which may enable you to score many sure points.

You learn how to confront new questions, or types of questions, and to attack them confidently and work out the correct answers.

You note objectives and emphases, and recognize pitfalls and dangers, so that you may make positive educational adjustments.

Moreover, you are kept fully informed in relation to new concepts, methods, practices, and directions in the field.

You discover that you arre actually taking the examination all the time: you are preparing for the examination by "taking" an examination, not by reading extraneous and/or supererogatory textbooks.

In short, this PASSBOOK®, used directedly, should be an important factor in helping you to pass your test.

BULK MAIL TECHNICIAN (USPS)

DUTIES

Accepts, verifies, classifies and computes postage on all classes of domestic and international business mail. Provides customer assistance to ensure understanding of postal mailing standards, mail preparation requirements and methods of presentation. Bulk Mail Technicians are responsible for carrying out the following duties:

- Providing customer education including advising customers as to proper mailing procedures, business mail preparation, postage payment systems and related requirements. Resolving customer complaints and inquiries, providing mailing options and necessary information to promote customer satisfaction;
- Accepting and verifying all classes of business mail presented at either postal or customer facilities, as required;
- Determining classification of all mail matter, weight and number of pieces, and computing postage and fees to be charged. Determining accuracy of postage statements. Reviewing customer accounts to ensure applicable fees are paid and checks availability of sufficient deposit by customer to cover cost of mailing. Releasing cleared mail to processing operations;
- Accepting deposits and write receipts. Maintaining records of permit holders, deposits, withdrawals and miscellaneous information for all classes of business mail. Completing necessary reports and submitting as directed;
- Utilizing a variety of business equipment for the collection, calculation, recording and reporting of all types of business mail entry data, including mail piece characteristics;
- Conducting training on business mail preparation, requirements and procedures to internal and external customers in a variety of on and off site locations. Participating in mailer meetings. May be required to be certified and serve as an on-the-job instructor;
- May assist management with duties such as scheduling, timekeeping and preparing administrative reports. May serve as liaison by keeping other employees current on present rulings, changes in rates, acceptance procedures or other related matters;
- May be required to accept, review, complete and process applications for all classes of mail; issue licenses and permits; notify customers of noncompliance, improper use, cancellations and revocations of licenses, permits, etc. and take appropriate action;
- May be required to perform audits and reviews for all classes of mail, both on and off site, and take appropriate action; and
- Performing other related duties as directed. May be required to separate and distribute mail that has been accepted, and perform general business mail entry administrative duties.

SCOPE OF THE EXAMINATION

Candidates are required to complete Virtual Entry Assessment Test CS (477), which includes exam sections on work scenarios (situational judgment); working a cash register; biodata questionnaire; and personality test.

VIRTUAL ENTRY ASSESSMENT TESTS
UNITED STATES POSTAL SERVICE

The Virtual Entry Assessment Tests are online assessments used by the United States Postal Service (USPS) to screen candidates for various positions. In April 2019, the USPS replaced Postal Exam 473 with four new exams:

- **Virtual Entry Assessment MC (474) - for Mail Carrier jobs**
- **Virtual Entry Assessment MH (475) - for Mail Handler jobs**
- **Virtual Entry Assessment MP (476) - for Mail Processing jobs**
- **Virtual Entry Assessment CS (477) - for Customer Service Clerk jobs**

The passing score for any of the four VEA tests is 70. Candidates who fail to reach the minimum score of 70 can retake the exam after one year. It is important to score as highly as possible (maximum score is 100) because candidates who achieve a passing score of 70 but do not get hired are ineligible to retake the exam for two years.

Virtual Entry Assessment Tests are self-administered and must be completed within three days of applying for a USPS job. Test results for each of the four assessments are used to fill a variety of Postal Service positions. For instance, scores on the Mail Carrier 474 exam will screen candidates for different levels of City Carrier and Rural Carrier jobs.

Virtual Entry Assessment MC (474)

Virtual Entry Assessment MC (474) is used for evaluating candidates applying for both City and Rural Carrier positions. The 474 exam is structured as follows:

Section Name	Number of Questions	Time Limit (approx.)
Work Scenarios (Situational Judgment)	9	7 minutes
Tell Us Your Story (Biodata Questionnaire)	20	2 minutes
Describe Your Approach (Personality Test)	56	6 minutes

SAMPLE QUESTION

Work Scenarios (Situational Judgment)
You are carrying mail outside an apartment building when a resident asks for the address of a nearby restaurant. He is not sure how to locate this information but inquired with the assumption you are familiar with the neighborhood.

Select the course of action you would most likely take in the work scenario described above.

    A. *Tell him he can find that information on a simple internet search*
    B. *Explain where he may find this information and follow up to see if he found it*
    C. *Offer to help him search for the address on the USPS website*
    D. *Tell him where he can find this information and ask if you can help in any other way*

Virtual Entry Assessment MH (475)

Virtual Entry Assessment MH 475 is an exam for candidates looking to become a USPS Mail Handler or Mail Handler Assistant. The 475 exam is structured as follows:

Section Name	Number of Questions	Time Limit (approx.)
Work Scenarios (Situational Judgment)	9	11 minutes
Check for Errors	12	2 minutes
Tell Us Your Story (Biodata Questionnaire)	22	3 minutes
Describe Your Approach	79	8 minutes

SAMPLE QUESTION

Check For Errors
Choose the option (A, B, C, or D) with the identification number and name that EXACTLY matches the number and name provided.

981121 Phillip M. Maas

    A. *981121 Phillip M. Mass*
    B. *981211 Phillip M. Maas*
    C. *981121 Phillip M. Maas*
    D. *981121 Phillip N. Maas*

Virtual Entry Assessment MP (476)

Virtual Entry Assessment MP 476 is used in the screening process for many roles related to Mail Processing, such as Clerks and Conversion Operators. The 476 exam is structured as follows:

Section Name	Number of Questions	Time Limit (approx.)
Work Scenarios (Situational Judgment)	9	11 minutes
Check for Errors	12	2 minutes
Tell Us Your Story (Biodata Questionnaire)	22	3 minutes
Describe Your Approach	79	8 minutes

Tell Us Your Story (Biodata Questionnaire)

After completing an important project ahead of schedule, which of the following gives you the GREATEST satisfaction?

    A. *Being told you have done a good job.*
    B. *Providing a solution that helps others.*
    C. *Innovating a new way to carry out or manage a project.*
    D. *Having free time to devote to personal interests.*

Virtual Entry Assessment CS (477)

Virtual Entry Assessment CS 477 is used to screen candidates for retail customer service jobs at the Post Office. The 477 exam is structured as follows:

Section Name	Number of Questions	Time Limit (approx.)
Work Scenarios (Situational Judgment)	10	8 minutes
Work Your Register	3	2 minutes
Tell Us Your Story (Biodata Questionnaire)	21	2 minutes
Describe Your Approach	56	6 minutes

SAMPLE QUESTION

Work Your Register

A customer hands you a $5 bill to pay for postage totaling $1.30. What is the CORRECT change listed below that you should give to the customer?

    D. *No change should be given*

HOW TO TAKE A TEST

I. YOU MUST PASS AN EXAMINATION

A. *WHAT EVERY CANDIDATE SHOULD KNOW*

Examination applicants often ask us for help in preparing for the written test. What can I study in advance? What kinds of questions will be asked? How will the test be given? How will the papers be graded?

As an applicant for a civil service examination, you may be wondering about some of these things. Our purpose here is to suggest effective methods of advance study and to describe civil service examinations.

Your chances for success on this examination can be increased if you know how to prepare. Those "pre-examination jitters" can be reduced if you know what to expect. You can even experience an adventure in good citizenship if you know why civil service exams are given.

B. *WHY ARE CIVIL SERVICE EXAMINATIONS GIVEN?*

Civil service examinations are important to you in two ways. As a citizen, you want public jobs filled by employees who know how to do their work. As a job seeker, you want a fair chance to compete for that job on an equal footing with other candidates. The best-known means of accomplishing this two-fold goal is the competitive examination.

Exams are widely publicized throughout the nation. They may be administered for jobs in federal, state, city, municipal, town or village governments or agencies.

Any citizen may apply, with some limitations, such as the age or residence of applicants. Your experience and education may be reviewed to see whether you meet the requirements for the particular examination. When these requirements exist, they are reasonable and applied consistently to all applicants. Thus, a competitive examination may cause you some uneasiness now, but it is your privilege and safeguard.

C. *HOW ARE CIVIL SERVICE EXAMS DEVELOPED?*

Examinations are carefully written by trained technicians who are specialists in the field known as "psychological measurement," in consultation with recognized authorities in the field of work that the test will cover. These experts recommend the subject matter areas or skills to be tested; only those knowledges or skills important to your success on the job are included. The most reliable books and source materials available are used as references. Together, the experts and technicians judge the difficulty level of the questions.

Test technicians know how to phrase questions so that the problem is clearly stated. Their ethics do not permit "trick" or "catch" questions. Questions may have been tried out on sample groups, or subjected to statistical analysis, to determine their usefulness.

Written tests are often used in combination with performance tests, ratings of training and experience, and oral interviews. All of these measures combine to form the best-known means of finding the right person for the right job.

II. HOW TO PASS THE WRITTEN TEST

A. NATURE OF THE EXAMINATION

To prepare intelligently for civil service examinations, you should know how they differ from school examinations you have taken. In school you were assigned certain definite pages to read or subjects to cover. The examination questions were quite detailed and usually emphasized memory. Civil service exams, on the other hand, try to discover your present ability to perform the duties of a position, plus your potentiality to learn these duties. In other words, a civil service exam attempts to predict how successful you will be. Questions cover such a broad area that they cannot be as minute and detailed as school exam questions.

In the public service similar kinds of work, or positions, are grouped together in one "class." This process is known as *position-classification*. All the positions in a class are paid according to the salary range for that class. One class title covers all of these positions, and they are all tested by the same examination.

B. FOUR BASIC STEPS

1) Study the announcement

How, then, can you know what subjects to study? Our best answer is: "Learn as much as possible about the class of positions for which you've applied." The exam will test the knowledge, skills and abilities needed to do the work.

Your most valuable source of information about the position you want is the official exam announcement. This announcement lists the training and experience qualifications. Check these standards and apply only if you come reasonably close to meeting them.

The brief description of the position in the examination announcement offers some clues to the subjects which will be tested. Think about the job itself. Review the duties in your mind. Can you perform them, or are there some in which you are rusty? Fill in the blank spots in your preparation.

Many jurisdictions preview the written test in the exam announcement by including a section called "Knowledge and Abilities Required," "Scope of the Examination," or some similar heading. Here you will find out specifically what fields will be tested.

2) Review your own background

Once you learn in general what the position is all about, and what you need to know to do the work, ask yourself which subjects you already know fairly well and which need improvement. You may wonder whether to concentrate on improving your strong areas or on building some background in your fields of weakness. When the announcement has specified "some knowledge" or "considerable knowledge," or has used adjectives like "beginning principles of..." or "advanced ... methods," you can get a clue as to the number and difficulty of questions to be asked in any given field. More questions, and hence broader coverage, would be included for those subjects which are more important in the work. Now weigh your strengths and weaknesses against the job requirements and prepare accordingly.

3) Determine the level of the position

Another way to tell how intensively you should prepare is to understand the level of the job for which you are applying. Is it the entering level? In other words, is this the position in which beginners in a field of work are hired? Or is it an intermediate or advanced level? Sometimes this is indicated by such words as "Junior" or "Senior" in the class title. Other jurisdictions use Roman numerals to designate the level – Clerk I, Clerk II, for example. The word "Supervisor" sometimes appears in the title. If the level is not indicated by the title, check the description of duties. Will you be working under very close supervision, or will you have responsibility for independent decisions in this work?

4) Choose appropriate study materials

Now that you know the subjects to be examined and the relative amount of each subject to be covered, you can choose suitable study materials. For beginning level jobs, or even advanced ones, if you have a pronounced weakness in some aspect of your training, read a modern, standard textbook in that field. Be sure it is up to date and has general coverage. Such books are normally available at your library, and the librarian will be glad to help you locate one. For entry-level positions, questions of appropriate difficulty are chosen – neither highly advanced questions, nor those too simple. Such questions require careful thought but not advanced training.

If the position for which you are applying is technical or advanced, you will read more advanced, specialized material. If you are already familiar with the basic principles of your field, elementary textbooks would waste your time. Concentrate on advanced textbooks and technical periodicals. Think through the concepts and review difficult problems in your field.

These are all general sources. You can get more ideas on your own initiative, following these leads. For example, training manuals and publications of the government agency which employs workers in your field can be useful, particularly for technical and professional positions. A letter or visit to the government department involved may result in more specific study suggestions, and certainly will provide you with a more definite idea of the exact nature of the position you are seeking.

III. KINDS OF TESTS

Tests are used for purposes other than measuring knowledge and ability to perform specified duties. For some positions, it is equally important to test ability to make adjustments to new situations or to profit from training. In others, basic mental abilities not dependent on information are essential. Questions which test these things may not appear as pertinent to the duties of the position as those which test for knowledge and information. Yet they are often highly important parts of a fair examination. For very general questions, it is almost impossible to help you direct your study efforts. What we can do is to point out some of the more common of these general abilities needed in public service positions and describe some typical questions.

1) General information

Broad, general information has been found useful for predicting job success in some kinds of work. This is tested in a variety of ways, from vocabulary lists to questions about current events. Basic background in some field of work, such as sociology or economics, may be sampled in a group of questions. Often these are principles which have become familiar to most persons through exposure rather than through formal training. It is difficult to advise you how to study for these questions; being alert to the world around you is our best suggestion.

2) Verbal ability

An example of an ability needed in many positions is verbal or language ability. Verbal ability is, in brief, the ability to use and understand words. Vocabulary and grammar tests are typical measures of this ability. Reading comprehension or paragraph interpretation questions are common in many kinds of civil service tests. You are given a paragraph of written material and asked to find its central meaning.

3) Numerical ability

Number skills can be tested by the familiar arithmetic problem, by checking paired lists of numbers to see which are alike and which are different, or by interpreting charts and graphs. In the latter test, a graph may be printed in the test booklet which you are asked to use as the basis for answering questions.

4) Observation

A popular test for law-enforcement positions is the observation test. A picture is shown to you for several minutes, then taken away. Questions about the picture test your ability to observe both details and larger elements.

5) Following directions

In many positions in the public service, the employee must be able to carry out written instructions dependably and accurately. You may be given a chart with several columns, each column listing a variety of information. The questions require you to carry out directions involving the information given in the chart.

6) Skills and aptitudes

Performance tests effectively measure some manual skills and aptitudes. When the skill is one in which you are trained, such as typing or shorthand, you can practice. These tests are often very much like those given in business school or high school courses. For many of the other skills and aptitudes, however, no short-time preparation can be made. Skills and abilities natural to you or that you have developed throughout your lifetime are being tested.

Many of the general questions just described provide all the data needed to answer the questions and ask you to use your reasoning ability to find the answers. Your best preparation for these tests, as well as for tests of facts and ideas, is to be at your physical and mental best. You, no doubt, have your own methods of getting into an exam-taking mood and keeping "in shape." The next section lists some ideas on this subject.

IV. KINDS OF QUESTIONS

Only rarely is the "essay" question, which you answer in narrative form, used in civil service tests. Civil service tests are usually of the short-answer type. Full instructions for answering these questions will be given to you at the examination. But in case this is your first experience with short-answer questions and separate answer sheets, here is what you need to know:

1) Multiple-choice Questions

Most popular of the short-answer questions is the "multiple choice" or "best answer" question. It can be used, for example, to test for factual knowledge, ability to solve problems or judgment in meeting situations found at work.

A multiple-choice question is normally one of three types—

- It can begin with an incomplete statement followed by several possible endings. You are to find the one ending which *best* completes the statement, although some of the others may not be entirely wrong.
- It can also be a complete statement in the form of a question which is answered by choosing one of the statements listed.
- It can be in the form of a problem – again you select the best answer.

Here is an example of a multiple-choice question with a discussion which should give you some clues as to the method for choosing the right answer:

When an employee has a complaint about his assignment, the action which will *best* help him overcome his difficulty is to
- A. discuss his difficulty with his coworkers
- B. take the problem to the head of the organization
- C. take the problem to the person who gave him the assignment
- D. say nothing to anyone about his complaint

In answering this question, you should study each of the choices to find which is best. Consider choice "A" – Certainly an employee may discuss his complaint with fellow employees, but no change or improvement can result, and the complaint remains unresolved. Choice "B" is a poor choice since the head of the organization probably does not know what assignment you have been given, and taking your problem to him is known as "going over the head" of the supervisor. The supervisor, or person who made the assignment, is the person who can clarify it or correct any injustice. Choice "C" is, therefore, correct. To say nothing, as in choice "D," is unwise. Supervisors have and interest in knowing the problems employees are facing, and the employee is seeking a solution to his problem.

2) True/False Questions

The "true/false" or "right/wrong" form of question is sometimes used. Here a complete statement is given. Your job is to decide whether the statement is right or wrong.

SAMPLE: A roaming cell-phone call to a nearby city costs less than a non-roaming call to a distant city.

This statement is wrong, or false, since roaming calls are more expensive.

This is not a complete list of all possible question forms, although most of the others are variations of these common types. You will always get complete directions for answering questions. Be sure you understand *how* to mark your answers – ask questions until you do.

V. RECORDING YOUR ANSWERS

Computer terminals are used more and more today for many different kinds of exams.

For an examination with very few applicants, you may be told to record your answers in the test booklet itself. Separate answer sheets are much more common. If this separate answer sheet is to be scored by machine – and this is often the case – it is highly important that you mark your answers correctly in order to get credit.

An electronic scoring machine is often used in civil service offices because of the speed with which papers can be scored. Machine-scored answer sheets must be marked with a pencil, which will be given to you. This pencil has a high graphite content which responds to the electronic scoring machine. As a matter of fact, stray dots may register as answers, so do not let your pencil rest on the answer sheet while you are pondering the correct answer. Also, if your pencil lead breaks or is otherwise defective, ask for another.

Since the answer sheet will be dropped in a slot in the scoring machine, be careful not to bend the corners or get the paper crumpled.

The answer sheet normally has five vertical columns of numbers, with 30 numbers to a column. These numbers correspond to the question numbers in your test booklet. After each number, going across the page are four or five pairs of dotted lines. These short dotted lines have small letters or numbers above them. The first two pairs may also have a "T" or "F" above the letters. This indicates that the first two pairs only are to be used if the questions are of the true-false type. If the questions are multiple choice, disregard the "T" and "F" and pay attention only to the small letters or numbers.

Answer your questions in the manner of the sample that follows:

32. The largest city in the United States is
    A. Washington, D.C.
    B. New York City
    C. Chicago
    D. Detroit
    E. San Francisco

1) Choose the answer you think is best. (New York City is the largest, so "B" is correct.)
2) Find the row of dotted lines numbered the same as the question you are answering. (Find row number 32)
3) Find the pair of dotted lines corresponding to the answer. (Find the pair of lines under the mark "B.")
4) Make a solid black mark between the dotted lines.

VI. BEFORE THE TEST

Common sense will help you find procedures to follow to get ready for an examination. Too many of us, however, overlook these sensible measures. Indeed, nervousness and fatigue have been found to be the most serious reasons why applicants fail to do their best on civil service tests. Here is a list of reminders:

- Begin your preparation early – Don't wait until the last minute to go scurrying around for books and materials or to find out what the position is all about.
- Prepare continuously – An hour a night for a week is better than an all-night cram session. This has been definitely established. What is more, a night a week for a month will return better dividends than crowding your study into a shorter period of time.
- Locate the place of the exam – You have been sent a notice telling you when and where to report for the examination. If the location is in a different town or otherwise unfamiliar to you, it would be well to inquire the best route and learn something about the building.
- Relax the night before the test – Allow your mind to rest. Do not study at all that night. Plan some mild recreation or diversion; then go to bed early and get a good night's sleep.
- Get up early enough to make a leisurely trip to the place for the test – This way unforeseen events, traffic snarls, unfamiliar buildings, etc. will not upset you.
- Dress comfortably – A written test is not a fashion show. You will be known by number and not by name, so wear something comfortable.
- Leave excess paraphernalia at home – Shopping bags and odd bundles will get in your way. You need bring only the items mentioned in the official notice you received; usually everything you need is provided. Do not bring reference books to the exam. They will only confuse those last minutes and be taken away from you when in the test room.
- Arrive somewhat ahead of time – If because of transportation schedules you must get there very early, bring a newspaper or magazine to take your mind off yourself while waiting.
- Locate the examination room – When you have found the proper room, you will be directed to the seat or part of the room where you will sit. Sometimes you are given a sheet of instructions to read while you are waiting. Do not fill out any forms until you are told to do so; just read them and be prepared.
- Relax and prepare to listen to the instructions
- If you have any physical problem that may keep you from doing your best, be sure to tell the test administrator. If you are sick or in poor health, you really cannot do your best on the exam. You can come back and take the test some other time.

VII. AT THE TEST

The day of the test is here and you have the test booklet in your hand. The temptation to get going is very strong. Caution! There is more to success than knowing the right answers. You must know how to identify your papers and understand variations in the type of short-answer question used in this particular examination. Follow these suggestions for maximum results from your efforts:

1) Cooperate with the monitor

The test administrator has a duty to create a situation in which you can be as much at ease as possible. He will give instructions, tell you when to begin, check to see that you are marking your answer sheet correctly, and so on. He is not there to guard you, although he will see that your competitors do not take unfair advantage. He wants to help you do your best.

2) Listen to all instructions

Don't jump the gun! Wait until you understand all directions. In most civil service tests you get more time than you need to answer the questions. So don't be in a hurry. Read each word of instructions until you clearly understand the meaning. Study the examples, listen to all announcements and follow directions. Ask questions if you do not understand what to do.

3) Identify your papers

Civil service exams are usually identified by number only. You will be assigned a number; you must not put your name on your test papers. Be sure to copy your number correctly. Since more than one exam may be given, copy your exact examination title.

4) Plan your time

Unless you are told that a test is a "speed" or "rate of work" test, speed itself is usually not important. Time enough to answer all the questions will be provided, but this does not mean that you have all day. An overall time limit has been set. Divide the total time (in minutes) by the number of questions to determine the approximate time you have for each question.

5) Do not linger over difficult questions

If you come across a difficult question, mark it with a paper clip (useful to have along) and come back to it when you have been through the booklet. One caution if you do this – be sure to skip a number on your answer sheet as well. Check often to be sure that you have not lost your place and that you are marking in the row numbered the same as the question you are answering.

6) Read the questions

Be sure you know what the question asks! Many capable people are unsuccessful because they failed to *read* the questions correctly.

7) Answer all questions

Unless you have been instructed that a penalty will be deducted for incorrect answers, it is better to guess than to omit a question.

8) Speed tests

It is often better NOT to guess on speed tests. It has been found that on timed tests people are tempted to spend the last few seconds before time is called in marking answers at random – without even reading them – in the hope of picking up a few extra points. To discourage this practice, the instructions may warn you that your score will be "corrected" for guessing. That is, a penalty will be applied. The incorrect answers will be deducted from the correct ones, or some other penalty formula will be used.

9) Review your answers
    If you finish before time is called, go back to the questions you guessed or omitted to give them further thought. Review other answers if you have time.

10) Return your test materials
    If you are ready to leave before others have finished or time is called, take ALL your materials to the monitor and leave quietly. Never take any test material with you. The monitor can discover whose papers are not complete, and taking a test booklet may be grounds for disqualification.

VIII. EXAMINATION TECHNIQUES

1) Read the general instructions carefully. These are usually printed on the first page of the exam booklet. As a rule, these instructions refer to the timing of the examination; the fact that you should not start work until the signal and must stop work at a signal, etc. If there are any *special* instructions, such as a choice of questions to be answered, make sure that you note this instruction carefully.

2) When you are ready to start work on the examination, that is as soon as the signal has been given, read the instructions to each question booklet, underline any key words or phrases, such as *least, best, outline, describe* and the like. In this way you will tend to answer as requested rather than discover on reviewing your paper that you *listed without describing*, that you selected the *worst* choice rather than the *best* choice, etc.

3) If the examination is of the objective or multiple-choice type – that is, each question will also give a series of possible answers: A, B, C or D, and you are called upon to select the best answer and write the letter next to that answer on your answer paper – it is advisable to start answering each question in turn. There may be anywhere from 50 to 100 such questions in the three or four hours allotted and you can see how much time would be taken if you read through all the questions before beginning to answer any. Furthermore, if you come across a question or group of questions which you know would be difficult to answer, it would undoubtedly affect your handling of all the other questions.

4) If the examination is of the essay type and contains but a few questions, it is a moot point as to whether you should read all the questions before starting to answer any one. Of course, if you are given a choice – say five out of seven and the like – then it is essential to read all the questions so you can eliminate the two that are most difficult. If, however, you are asked to answer all the questions, there may be danger in trying to answer the easiest one first because you may find that you will spend too much time on it. The best technique is to answer the first question, then proceed to the second, etc.

5) Time your answers. Before the exam begins, write down the time it started, then add the time allowed for the examination and write down the time it must be completed, then divide the time available somewhat as follows:

- If 3-1/2 hours are allowed, that would be 210 minutes. If you have 80 objective-type questions, that would be an average of 2-1/2 minutes per question. Allow yourself no more than 2 minutes per question, or a total of 160 minutes, which will permit about 50 minutes to review.
- If for the time allotment of 210 minutes there are 7 essay questions to answer, that would average about 30 minutes a question. Give yourself only 25 minutes per question so that you have about 35 minutes to review.

6) The most important instruction is to *read each question* and make sure you know what is wanted. The second most important instruction is to *time yourself properly* so that you answer every question. The third most important instruction is to *answer every question*. Guess if you have to but include something for each question. Remember that you will receive no credit for a blank and will probably receive some credit if you write something in answer to an essay question. If you guess a letter – say "B" for a multiple-choice question – you may have guessed right. If you leave a blank as an answer to a multiple-choice question, the examiners may respect your feelings but it will not add a point to your score. Some exams may penalize you for wrong answers, so in such cases *only*, you may not want to guess unless you have some basis for your answer.

7) Suggestions
   a. Objective-type questions
      1. Examine the question booklet for proper sequence of pages and questions
      2. Read all instructions carefully
      3. Skip any question which seems too difficult; return to it after all other questions have been answered
      4. Apportion your time properly; do not spend too much time on any single question or group of questions
      5. Note and underline key words – *all, most, fewest, least, best, worst, same, opposite,* etc.
      6. Pay particular attention to negatives
      7. Note unusual option, e.g., unduly long, short, complex, different or similar in content to the body of the question
      8. Observe the use of "hedging" words – *probably, may, most likely,* etc.
      9. Make sure that your answer is put next to the same number as the question
      10. Do not second-guess unless you have good reason to believe the second answer is definitely more correct
      11. Cross out original answer if you decide another answer is more accurate; do not erase until you are ready to hand your paper in
      12. Answer all questions; guess unless instructed otherwise
      13. Leave time for review

   b. Essay questions
      1. Read each question carefully
      2. Determine exactly what is wanted. Underline key words or phrases.
      3. Decide on outline or paragraph answer

4. Include many different points and elements unless asked to develop any one or two points or elements
5. Show impartiality by giving pros and cons unless directed to select one side only
6. Make and write down any assumptions you find necessary to answer the questions
7. Watch your English, grammar, punctuation and choice of words
8. Time your answers; don't crowd material

8) Answering the essay question

Most essay questions can be answered by framing the specific response around several key words or ideas. Here are a few such key words or ideas:

M's: manpower, materials, methods, money, management
P's: purpose, program, policy, plan, procedure, practice, problems, pitfalls, personnel, public relations
    a. Six basic steps in handling problems:
        1. Preliminary plan and background development
        2. Collect information, data and facts
        3. Analyze and interpret information, data and facts
        4. Analyze and develop solutions as well as make recommendations
        5. Prepare report and sell recommendations
        6. Install recommendations and follow up effectiveness

    b. Pitfalls to avoid
        1. *Taking things for granted* – A statement of the situation does not necessarily imply that each of the elements is necessarily true; for example, a complaint may be invalid and biased so that all that can be taken for granted is that a complaint has been registered
        2. *Considering only one side of a situation* – Wherever possible, indicate several alternatives and then point out the reasons you selected the best one
        3. *Failing to indicate follow up* – Whenever your answer indicates action on your part, make certain that you will take proper follow-up action to see how successful your recommendations, procedures or actions turn out to be
        4. *Taking too long in answering any single question* – Remember to time your answers properly

IX. AFTER THE TEST

Scoring procedures differ in detail among civil service jurisdictions although the general principles are the same. Whether the papers are hand-scored or graded by machine we have described, they are nearly always graded by number. That is, the person who marks the paper knows only the number – never the name – of the applicant. Not until all the papers have been graded will they be matched with names. If other tests, such as training and experience or oral interview ratings have been given, scores will be combined. Different parts of the examination usually have different weights. For example, the written test might count 60 percent of the final grade, and a rating of training and experience 40 percent. In many jurisdictions, veterans will have a certain number of points added to their grades.

After the final grade has been determined, the names are placed in grade order and an eligible list is established. There are various methods for resolving ties between those who get the same final grade – probably the most common is to place first the name of the person whose application was received first. Job offers are made from the eligible list in the order the names appear on it. You will be notified of your grade and your rank as soon as all these computations have been made. This will be done as rapidly as possible.

People who are found to meet the requirements in the announcement are called "eligibles." Their names are put on a list of eligible candidates. An eligible's chances of getting a job depend on how high he stands on this list and how fast agencies are filling jobs from the list.

When a job is to be filled from a list of eligibles, the agency asks for the names of people on the list of eligibles for that job. When the civil service commission receives this request, it sends to the agency the names of the three people highest on this list. Or, if the job to be filled has specialized requirements, the office sends the agency the names of the top three persons who meet these requirements from the general list.

The appointing officer makes a choice from among the three people whose names were sent to him. If the selected person accepts the appointment, the names of the others are put back on the list to be considered for future openings.

That is the rule in hiring from all kinds of eligible lists, whether they are for typist, carpenter, chemist, or something else. For every vacancy, the appointing officer has his choice of any one of the top three eligibles on the list. This explains why the person whose name is on top of the list sometimes does not get an appointment when some of the persons lower on the list do. If the appointing officer chooses the second or third eligible, the No. 1 eligible does not get a job at once, but stays on the list until he is appointed or the list is terminated.

X. HOW TO PASS THE INTERVIEW TEST

The examination for which you applied requires an oral interview test. You have already taken the written test and you are now being called for the interview test – the final part of the formal examination.

You may think that it is not possible to prepare for an interview test and that there are no procedures to follow during an interview. Our purpose is to point out some things you can do in advance that will help you and some good rules to follow and pitfalls to avoid while you are being interviewed.

What is an interview supposed to test?

The written examination is designed to test the technical knowledge and competence of the candidate; the oral is designed to evaluate intangible qualities, not readily measured otherwise, and to establish a list showing the relative fitness of each candidate – as measured against his competitors – for the position sought. Scoring is not on the basis of "right" and "wrong," but on a sliding scale of values ranging from "not passable" to "outstanding." As a matter of fact, it is possible to achieve a relatively low score without a single "incorrect" answer because of evident weakness in the qualities being measured.

Occasionally, an examination may consist entirely of an oral test – either an individual or a group oral. In such cases, information is sought concerning the technical knowledges and abilities of the candidate, since there has been no written examination for this purpose. More commonly, however, an oral test is used to supplement a written examination.

Who conducts interviews?

The composition of oral boards varies among different jurisdictions. In nearly all, a representative of the personnel department serves as chairman. One of the members of the board may be a representative of the department in which the candidate would work. In some cases, "outside experts" are used, and, frequently, a businessman or some other representative of the general public is asked to serve. Labor and management or other special groups may be represented. The aim is to secure the services of experts in the appropriate field.

However the board is composed, it is a good idea (and not at all improper or unethical) to ascertain in advance of the interview who the members are and what groups they represent. When you are introduced to them, you will have some idea of their backgrounds and interests, and at least you will not stutter and stammer over their names.

What should be done before the interview?

While knowledge about the board members is useful and takes some of the surprise element out of the interview, there is other preparation which is more substantive. It *is* possible to prepare for an oral interview – in several ways:

1) Keep a copy of your application and review it carefully before the interview

This may be the only document before the oral board, and the starting point of the interview. Know what education and experience you have listed there, and the sequence and dates of all of it. Sometimes the board will ask you to review the highlights of your experience for them; you should not have to hem and haw doing it.

2) Study the class specification and the examination announcement

Usually, the oral board has one or both of these to guide them. The qualities, characteristics or knowledges required by the position sought are stated in these documents. They offer valuable clues as to the nature of the oral interview. For example, if the job involves supervisory responsibilities, the announcement will usually indicate that knowledge of modern supervisory methods and the qualifications of the candidate as a supervisor will be tested. If so, you can expect such questions, frequently in the form of a hypothetical situation which you are expected to solve. NEVER go into an oral without knowledge of the duties and responsibilities of the job you seek.

3) Think through each qualification required

Try to visualize the kind of questions you would ask if you were a board member. How well could you answer them? Try especially to appraise your own knowledge and background in each area, *measured against the job sought*, and identify any areas in which you are weak. Be critical and realistic – do not flatter yourself.

4) Do some general reading in areas in which you feel you may be weak

For example, if the job involves supervision and your past experience has NOT, some general reading in supervisory methods and practices, particularly in the field of human relations, might be useful. Do NOT study agency procedures or detailed manuals. The oral board will be testing your understanding and capacity, not your memory.

5) Get a good night's sleep and watch your general health and mental attitude

You will want a clear head at the interview. Take care of a cold or any other minor ailment, and of course, no hangovers.

What should be done on the day of the interview?

Now comes the day of the interview itself. Give yourself plenty of time to get there. Plan to arrive somewhat ahead of the scheduled time, particularly if your appointment is in the fore part of the day. If a previous candidate fails to appear, the board might be ready for you a bit early. By early afternoon an oral board is almost invariably behind schedule if there are many candidates, and you may have to wait. Take along a book or magazine to read, or your application to review, but leave any extraneous material in the waiting room when you go in for your interview. In any event, relax and compose yourself.

The matter of dress is important. The board is forming impressions about you – from your experience, your manners, your attitude, and your appearance. Give your personal appearance careful attention. Dress your best, but not your flashiest. Choose conservative, appropriate clothing, and be sure it is immaculate. This is a business interview, and your appearance should indicate that you regard it as such. Besides, being well groomed and properly dressed will help boost your confidence.

Sooner or later, someone will call your name and escort you into the interview room. *This is it.* From here on you are on your own. It is too late for any more preparation. But remember, you asked for this opportunity to prove your fitness, and you are here because your request was granted.

What happens when you go in?

The usual sequence of events will be as follows: The clerk (who is often the board stenographer) will introduce you to the chairman of the oral board, who will introduce you to the other members of the board. Acknowledge the introductions before you sit down. Do not be surprised if you find a microphone facing you or a stenotypist sitting by. Oral interviews are usually recorded in the event of an appeal or other review.

Usually the chairman of the board will open the interview by reviewing the highlights of your education and work experience from your application – primarily for the benefit of the other members of the board, as well as to get the material into the record. Do not interrupt or comment unless there is an error or significant misinterpretation; if that is the case, do not hesitate. But do not quibble about insignificant matters. Also, he will usually ask you some question about your education, experience or your present job – partly to get you to start talking and to establish the interviewing "rapport." He may start the actual questioning, or turn it over to one of the other members. Frequently, each member undertakes the questioning on a particular area, one in which he is perhaps most competent, so you can expect each member to participate in the examination. Because time is limited, you may also expect some rather abrupt switches in the direction the questioning takes, so do not be upset by it. Normally, a board member will not pursue a single line of questioning unless he discovers a particular strength or weakness.

After each member has participated, the chairman will usually ask whether any member has any further questions, then will ask you if you have anything you wish to add. Unless you are expecting this question, it may floor you. Worse, it may start you off on an extended, extemporaneous speech. The board is not usually seeking more information. The question is principally to offer you a last opportunity to present further qualifications or to indicate that you have nothing to add. So, if you feel that a significant qualification or characteristic has been overlooked, it is proper to point it out in a sentence or so. Do not compliment the board on the thoroughness of their examination – they have been sketchy, and you know it. If you wish, merely say, "No thank you, I have nothing further to add." This is a point where you can "talk yourself out" of a good impression or fail to present an important bit of information. Remember, *you close the interview yourself.*

The chairman will then say, "That is all, Mr. _____, thank you." Do not be startled; the interview is over, and quicker than you think. Thank him, gather your belongings and take your leave. Save your sigh of relief for the other side of the door.

How to put your best foot forward

Throughout this entire process, you may feel that the board individually and collectively is trying to pierce your defenses, seek out your hidden weaknesses and embarrass and confuse you. Actually, this is not true. They are obliged to make an appraisal of your qualifications for the job you are seeking, and they want to see you in your best light. Remember, they must interview all candidates and a non-cooperative candidate may become a failure in spite of their best efforts to bring out his qualifications. Here are 15 suggestions that will help you:

1) Be natural – Keep your attitude confident, not cocky

If you are not confident that you can do the job, do not expect the board to be. Do not apologize for your weaknesses, try to bring out your strong points. The board is interested in a positive, not negative, presentation. Cockiness will antagonize any board member and make him wonder if you are covering up a weakness by a false show of strength.

2) Get comfortable, but don't lounge or sprawl

Sit erectly but not stiffly. A careless posture may lead the board to conclude that you are careless in other things, or at least that you are not impressed by the importance of the occasion. Either conclusion is natural, even if incorrect. Do not fuss with your clothing, a pencil or an ashtray. Your hands may occasionally be useful to emphasize a point; do not let them become a point of distraction.

3) Do not wisecrack or make small talk

This is a serious situation, and your attitude should show that you consider it as such. Further, the time of the board is limited – they do not want to waste it, and neither should you.

4) Do not exaggerate your experience or abilities

In the first place, from information in the application or other interviews and sources, the board may know more about you than you think. Secondly, you probably will not get away with it. An experienced board is rather adept at spotting such a situation, so do not take the chance.

5) If you know a board member, do not make a point of it, yet do not hide it

Certainly you are not fooling him, and probably not the other members of the board. Do not try to take advantage of your acquaintanceship – it will probably do you little good.

6) Do not dominate the interview

Let the board do that. They will give you the clues – do not assume that you have to do all the talking. Realize that the board has a number of questions to ask you, and do not try to take up all the interview time by showing off your extensive knowledge of the answer to the first one.

7) Be attentive

You only have 20 minutes or so, and you should keep your attention at its sharpest throughout. When a member is addressing a problem or question to you, give him your undivided attention. Address your reply principally to him, but do not exclude the other board members.

8) Do not interrupt

A board member may be stating a problem for you to analyze. He will ask you a question when the time comes. Let him state the problem, and wait for the question.

9) Make sure you understand the question

Do not try to answer until you are sure what the question is. If it is not clear, restate it in your own words or ask the board member to clarify it for you. However, do not haggle about minor elements.

10) Reply promptly but not hastily

A common entry on oral board rating sheets is "candidate responded readily," or "candidate hesitated in replies." Respond as promptly and quickly as you can, but do not jump to a hasty, ill-considered answer.

11) Do not be peremptory in your answers

A brief answer is proper – but do not fire your answer back. That is a losing game from your point of view. The board member can probably ask questions much faster than you can answer them.

12) Do not try to create the answer you think the board member wants

He is interested in what kind of mind you have and how it works – not in playing games. Furthermore, he can usually spot this practice and will actually grade you down on it.

13) Do not switch sides in your reply merely to agree with a board member

Frequently, a member will take a contrary position merely to draw you out and to see if you are willing and able to defend your point of view. Do not start a debate, yet do not surrender a good position. If a position is worth taking, it is worth defending.

14) Do not be afraid to admit an error in judgment if you are shown to be wrong

The board knows that you are forced to reply without any opportunity for careful consideration. Your answer may be demonstrably wrong. If so, admit it and get on with the interview.

15) Do not dwell at length on your present job

The opening question may relate to your present assignment. Answer the question but do not go into an extended discussion. You are being examined for a *new* job, not your present one. As a matter of fact, try to phrase ALL your answers in terms of the job for which you are being examined.

Basis of Rating

Probably you will forget most of these "do's" and "don'ts" when you walk into the oral interview room. Even remembering them all will not ensure you a passing grade. Perhaps you did not have the qualifications in the first place. But remembering them will help you to put your best foot forward, without treading on the toes of the board members.

Rumor and popular opinion to the contrary notwithstanding, an oral board wants you to make the best appearance possible. They know you are under pressure – but they also want to see how you respond to it as a guide to what your reaction would be under the pressures of the job you seek. They will be influenced by the degree of poise you display, the personal traits you show and the manner in which you respond.

ABOUT THIS BOOK

This book contains tests divided into Examination Sections. Go through each test, answering every question in the margin. At the end of each test look at the answer key and check your answers. On the ones you got wrong, look at the right answer choice and learn. Do not fill in the answers first. Do not memorize the questions and answers, but understand the answer and principles involved. On your test, the questions will likely be different from the samples. Questions are changed and new ones added. If you understand these past questions you should have success with any changes that arise. Tests may consist of several types of questions. We have additional books on each subject should more study be advisable or necessary for you. Finally, the more you study, the better prepared you will be. This book is intended to be the last thing you study before you walk into the examination room. Prior study of relevant texts is also recommended. NLC publishes some of these in our Fundamental Series. Knowledge and good sense are important factors in passing your exam. Good luck also helps. So now study this Passbook, absorb the material contained within and take that knowledge into the examination. Then do your best to pass that exam.

EXAMINATION SECTION

SITUATIONAL JUDGMENT

These questions test for the ability to identify appropriate and effective responses to work-related challenges. You will be presented with a scenario that reflects the types of challenges one could encounter in a work environment. Each scenario will be followed by several responses to the scenario. You must rate the effectiveness of each response to the given scenario.

EXAMPLES OF USE ON THE JOB: Law enforcement officers must use situational judgment in performing daily work activities including, but not limited to, interacting with colleagues and the public, responding to emergencies or dangerous situations, making arrests, and questioning suspects and witnesses.

TEST TASK: You will be presented with a description of realistic, job-related situations that law enforcement officers may encounter. Each situation is followed by several responses. Each response consists of an action or actions taken in response to the situation. You will be asked to rate the level of effectiveness of EACH response provided using the scale below. Please note that each response is independent from the others; therefore, **you may select the same effectiveness rating for more than one response to a particular situation.** No previous knowledge of the job is required to answer these questions.

SAMPLE QUESTIONS:

Very Ineffective	Ineffective	Effective	Very Effective
A	B	C	S

Choice A (Very Ineffective): Select this choice if you believe the response <u>does not</u> address the situation at hand and responding in this way could create additional problems or could make the situation worse.

Choice B (Ineffective): Select this choice if you believe the response as a whole <u>does not</u> adequately address the situation at hand.

Choice C (Effective): Select this choice if you believe the response as a whole adequately addresses the situation at hand.

Choice D (Very Effective): Select this choice if you believe the response addresses the situation at hand in a superior manner.

SITUATION: A junior officer is confronted with a difficult task and there is no one available to assist him with this task. The task urgently needs to be completed and, while difficult, it ca be safely completed individually.

1. RESPONSE: The officer does his best to immediately address the task to the best of his ability.
   How would you rate this response to the situation above?
   A. Very Ineffective
   B. Ineffective
   C. Effective
   D. Very Effective

2. RESPONSE: The officer ignores the urgency of the task and waits until another more senior officer is available to assist him.
   How would you rate this response to the situation above?
   A. Very Ineffective
   B. Ineffective
   C. Effective
   D. Very Effective

3. RESPONSE: The officer ignores the task all together.
   How would you rate this response to the situation above?
   A. Very Ineffective
   B. Ineffective
   C. Effective
   D. Very Effective

4. RESPONSE: The officer performs the task in a less-than-perfect manner to get it done as quickly as possible.
   How would you rate this response to the situation above?
   A. Very Ineffective
   B. Ineffective
   C. Effective
   D. Very Effective

DISCUSSION: Please note that you may assign "very ineffective," "ineffective," "effective," and "very effective" multiple times for each situation. For example, in the sample question above, if you believe both responses 1 and 4 are "effective" responses, you would select choice C for both number 1 and number 4. Similarly, if you believe that both responses 2 and 3 are "ineffective" responses, you would select choice B as an answer for both numbers 2 and 3.

SITUATIONAL JUDGMENT TIPS: The scenarios presented in the exam are described within the context of the police officer job; however, it is important to note that none of these questions require you to have any knowledge of law enforcement practices or conventions. While these are hypothetical situations, you should rate the effectiveness of each response as though they are real actions taken in response to real events.

_____

EXAMINATION SECTION
TEST 1

DIRECTIONS: Each question or incomplete statement is followed by several suggested answers or completions. Select the one that BEST answers the question or completes the statement. *PRINT THE LETTER OF THE CORRECT ANSWER IN THE SPACE AT THE RIGHT.*

1. In considering a new word processing system for a regional office, which of the following would MOST likely be the MOST important consideration in making a decision?   1.____

   A. Ease of operation
   B. Friendliness of service technicians
   C. Availability of service technicians
   D. Capacity of the system to meet the unit's word processing needs

2. Your supervisor is out of town for several days and has asked you to act as supervisor in his absence. An employee in the unit comes to you and complains that the supervisor has been dividing the workload unfairly.   2.____
   Of the following, the MOST appropriate action for you to take is

   A. defend the actions of your supervisor
   B. encourage the employee to file a grievance
   C. listen to the employee attentively
   D. explain to the employee that you have no authority to handle the situation

3. A principal stenographer still on probation is instructed to supervise and coordinate the completion of a large word processing project. Her supervisor asks her how long she thinks the project will take. The principal stenographer gives her supervisor an estimate that is two days longer than she actually thinks the project will take to complete. The project is completed two days earlier, and the principal stenographer is congratulated by her supervisor for her efforts.   3.____
   In purposely overestimating the time required to complete the project, the principal stenographer showed

   A. *good* judgment because it helped her appear very efficient
   B. *good* judgment because it helps keep unrealistic supervisors from expecting too much
   C. *poor* judgment because plans and schedules of other components of the project may have been based on her false estimate
   D. *poor* judgment because she should have used the extra time to further check and, proofread the work

4. Which of the following would MOST likely be the MOST important in providing support to one's supervisor?   4.____

   A. Screening annoying phone calls
   B. Reviewing and forwarding articles and publications that may be of interest to your supervisor
   C. Correctly transmitting instructions from the supervisor to appropriate staff members
   D. Reviewing outgoing correspondence for proper grammatical usage and clarity

5. While you are on the telephone answering a question about your agency, a visitor comes   5.___
to your desk and starts to ask you a question. There is no emergency or urgency in either
situation, that of the phone call or that of answering the visitor's question.
In this case, you should

    A. excuse yourself to the person on the telephone and tell the visitor that you will be
with him or her as soon as you have finished on the phone
    B. explain to the person on the phone that you have a visitor and must shorten the
conversation
    C. continue to talk with the person on the phone while looking up occasionally at the
visitor to let him or her know that you know he or she is there
    D. continue to talk with the person on the telephone until you are finished and then let
the visitor know that you're sorry to have kept him or her waiting

6. Your supervisor is out of town on vacation for one week, and asks you to act as supervi-   6.___
sor in her absence. The second day she is gone a very important, complex budgetary
form, which must be responded to in ten days, arrives in your unit.
Of the following, it would be BEST if you

    A. filled out the form and submitted it as soon as possible
    B. read the form over, did any time-consuming research that might be needed, and
then gave the uncompleted form to your supervisor as soon as she returned
    C. asked for help from your supervisor's supervisor in completing the form
    D. tried to contact your supervisor for advice

7. Of the following, which would MOST likely be of the highest priority?   7.___
The typing of

    A. a grant proposal due next week
    B. new addresses onto a mailing list for a future mailing
    C. a payroll form for a new employee that needs to be submitted immediately
    D. a memorandum from the Commissioner to all employees regarding new proce-
dures

8. Your office is moving to a new location.   8.___
Of the following, it would be MOST important to ensure that

    A. others will know your office's new address and phone number
    B. the new office space is comfortable
    C. your supervisor is happy with his or her new office space
    D. the move itself goes smoothly

9. Of the following, which would generally be considered the LEAST desirable?   9.___

    A. Accidentally disconnecting an executive from an important phone call
    B. Ordering the wrong back-up part for a copying machine
    C. Misplacing several hundred dollars worth of personal checks payable to your
department
    D. Misplacing a memorandum that needs to be typed

10. Your supervisor has told you not to let anyone disturb her for the rest of the morning unless absolutely necessary because she has some urgent work to complete. The department head telephones and asks to speak to her.
The BEST course of action for you to take is to

    A. ask the department head if he or she can leave a message
    B. ask your supervisor if she can take the call
    C. tell the department head that your supervisor is out
    D. let your supervisor know that her instructions have put you in a difficult position

10.____

11. Which of the following would be MOST likely to contribute to efficiency in the operation of an office?

    A. A new computer system is instituted in an office.
    B. The employees are paid well.
    C. Procedures and practices are studied for any redundant operations.
    D. A supervisor delegates work.

11.____

12. You are at work at your desk on a special project when a visitor approaches you. You cannot interrupt your work to take care of this person.
Of the following, the BEST and MOST courteous way of handling this situation is to

    A. avoid looking up from your work until you are finished with what you are doing
    B. tell the visitor that you will not be able to assist him or her for quite some time
    C. refer the individual to another employee who can take care of him or her right away
    D. chat with the individual while you continue to work

12.____

13. Which of the following would MOST likely be of the highest priority?
A(n)

    A. annual report due next month
    B. irate member of the public who is standing at your desk
    C. important financial report requested by the Commissioner
    D. memorandum to all employees outlining very important new policy needs to be typed and distributed immediately

13.____

14. Someone uses *special pull* to obtain the services of your unit at the last minute. You and the four employees you supervise have done everything you could do to provide good service, and you feel things have gone very well. The client is not pleased, however, and enters your office and begins screaming at you and the other employees present.
Of the following, it would be BEST if you

    A. ignored the person
    B. tried to calm the person down
    C. asked the person to leave the office
    D. called your supervisor in to help handle the situation

14.____

15. Your supervisor is on vacation for two weeks, and you have been asked to fill in for her.   15.____
Your office is very busy, and there is a strict procedure for filling requests. Leslie from Unit
X wants something completed immediately. You don't feel this is possible or reasonable,
and politely explain why to Leslie. Leslie becomes very angry and says that she will complain to your supervisor about your uncooperative behavior as soon as your supervisor
returns.
Of the following, it would be BEST if you

    A. filled Leslie's request
    B. reported Leslie to her supervisor
    C. complained to your supervisor about the situation as soon as she returned
    D. stood by your decision once you determined it was correct

---

KEY (CORRECT ANSWERS)

1. D	6. B	11. C
2. C	7. C	12. C
3. C	8. A	13. B
4. C	9. C	14. B
5. A	10. B	15. D

EXAMINATION SECTION
TEST 1

DIRECTIONS: Each question or incomplete statement is followed by several suggested answers or completions. Select the one that BEST answers the question or completes the statement. *PRINT THE LETTER OF THE CORRECT ANSWER IN THE SPACE AT THE RIGHT.*

1. If you open a personal letter by mistake, the one of the following actions which it would generally be BEST for you to take is to   1.____

    A. ignore your error, attach the envelope to the letter, and distribute in the usual manner
    B. personally give the addressee the letter without any explanation
    C. place the letter inside the envelope, indicate under your initials that it was opened in error, and give to the addressee
    D. reseal the envelope or place the contents in another envelope and pass on to addressee

2. If you receive a telephone call regarding a matter which your office does not handle, you should FIRST   2.____

    A. give the caller the telephone number of the proper office so that he can dial again
    B. offer to transfer the caller to the proper office
    C. suggest that the caller re-dial since he probably dialed incorrectly
    D. tell the caller he has reached the wrong office and then hang up

3. When you answer the telephone, the MOST important reason for identifying yourself and your organization is to   3.____

    A. give the caller time to collect his or her thoughts
    B. impress the caller with your courtesy
    C. inform the caller that he or she has reached the right number
    D. set a business-like tone at the beginning of the conversation

4. The one of the following cases in which you would NOT place a special notation in the left margin of a letter that you have typed is when   4.____

    A. one of the copies is intended for someone other than the addressee of the letter
    B. you enclose a flyer with the letter
    C. you sign your superior's name to the letter, at his or her request
    D. the letter refers to something being sent under separate cover

5. Suppose that you accidentally cut a letter or enclosure as you are opening an envelope with a paper knife.
The one of the following that you should do FIRST is to   5.____

    A. determine whether the document is important
    B. clip or staple the pieces together and process as usual
    C. mend the cut document with transparent tape
    D. notify the sender that the communication was damaged and request another copy

6. As soon as you pick up the phone, a very angry caller begins immediately to complain   6.__
   about city agencies and *red tape*. He says that he has been shifted to two or three different offices. It turns out that he is seeking information which is not immediately available
   to you. You believe you know, however, where it can be found.
   Which of the following actions is the BEST one for you to take?

   A. To eliminate all confusion, suggest that the caller write the mayor stating explicitly
      what he wants.
   B. Apologize by telling the caller how busy city agencies now are, but also tell him
      directly that you do not have the information he needs.
   C. Ask for the caller's telephone number, and assure him you will call back after you
      have checked further.
   D. Give the caller the name and telephone number of the person who might be able to
      help, but explain that you are not positive he will get results.

7. Suppose that one of your duties is to dictate responses to routine requests from the pub-   7.__
   lic for information. A letter writer asks for information which, as expressed in a one-sen-
   tence, explicit agency rule, cannot be given out to the public.
   Of the following ways of answering the letter, which is the MOST efficient?

   A. Quote verbatim that section of the agency rules which prohibits giving this informa-
      tion to the public.
   B. Without quoting the rule, explain why you cannot accede to the request and sug-
      gest alternative sources.
   C. Describe how carefully the request was considered before classifying it as subject
      to the rule forbidding the issuance of such information.
   D. Acknowledge receipt of the letter and advise that the requested information is not
      released to the public.

8. Suppose you assist in supervising a staff which has rather high morale, and your own   8.__
   supervisor asks you to poll the staff to find out who will be able to work overtime this particular evening to help complete emergency work.
   Which of the following approaches would be MOST likely to win their cooperation while
   maintaining their morale?

   A. Tell them that the better assignments will be given only to those who work over-
      time.
   B. Tell them that occasional overtime is a job requirement.
   C. Assure them they'll be doing you a personal favor.
   D. Let them know clearly why the overtime is needed.

9. Suppose that you have been asked to write and to prepare for reproduction new depart-   9.__
   mental vacation leave regulations.
   After you have written the new regulations, all of which fit on two pages, which one of
   the following would be the BEST method of reproducing 1,000 copies?

   A. An outside private printer because you can best maintain confidentiality using this
      technique
   B. Photocopying because the copies will have the best possible appearance
   C. Sending the file to all department employees as printable PDFs
   D. Printing and collating on the office high-volume printer

10. You are in charge of verifying employees' qualifications. This involves telephoning previous employers and schools. One of the applications which you are reviewing contains information which you are almost certain is correct on the basis of what the employee has told you.
The BEST thing to do is to

    A. check the information again with the employer
    B. perform the required verification procedures
    C. accept the information as valid
    D. ask a superior to verify the information

10._____

11. The practice of immediately identifying oneself and one's place of employment when contacting persons on the telephone is

    A. *good* because the receiver of the call can quickly identify the caller and establish a frame of reference
    B. *good* because it helps to set the caller at ease with the other party
    C. *poor* because it is not necessary to divulge that information when making general calls
    D. *poor* because it takes longer to arrive at the topic to be discussed

11._____

12. Which one of the following should be the MOST important overall consideration when preparing a recommendation to automate a large-scale office activity?
The

    A. number of models of automated equipment available
    B. benefits and costs of automation
    C. fears and resistance of affected employees
    D. experience of offices which have automated similar activities

12._____

13. A tickler file is MOST appropriate for filing materials

    A. chronologically according to date they were received
    B. alphabetically by name
    C. alphabetically by subject
    D. chronologically according to date they should be followed up

13._____

14. Which of the following is the BEST reason for decentralizing rather then centralizing the use of duplicating machines?

    A. Developing and retaining efficient duplicating machine operators
    B. Facilitating supervision of duplicating services
    C. Motivating employees to produce legible duplicated copies
    D. Placing the duplicating machines where they are most convenient and most frequently used

14._____

15. Window envelopes are sometimes considered preferable to individually addressed envelopes PRIMARILY because

    A. window envelopes are available in standard sizes for all purposes
    B. window envelopes are more attractive and official-looking
    C. the use of window envelopes eliminates the risk of inserting a letter in the wrong envelope
    D. the use of window envelopes requires neater typing

15._____

16. In planning the layout of a new office, the utilization of space and the arrangement of staff, furnishings, and equipment should usually be MOST influenced by the

    A. gross square footage
    B. status differences in the chain of command
    C. framework of informal relationships among employees
    D. activities to be performed

16.____

17. Office forms sometimes consist of several copies, each of a different color. The MAIN reason for using different colors is to

    A. make a favorable impression on the users of the form
    B. distinguish each copy from the others
    C. facilitate the preparation of legible carbon copies
    D. reduce cost, since using colored stock permits recycling of paper

17.____

18. Which of the following is the BEST justification for obtaining a photocopying machine for the office?

    A. A photocopying machine can produce an unlimited number of copies at a low fixed cost per copy.
    B. Employees need little training in operating a photocopying machine.
    C. Office costs will be reduced and efficiency increased.
    D. The legibility of a photocopy generally is superior to copy produced by any other office duplicating device.

18.____

19. An administrative officer in charge of a small fund for buying office supplies has just written a check to Charles Laird, a supplier, and has sent the check by messenger to him. A half-hour later, the messenger telephones the administrative officer. He has lost the check.
Which of the following is the MOST important action for the administrative officer to take under these circumstances?

    A. Ask the messenger to return and write a report describing the loss of the check.
    B. Make a note on the performance record of the messenger who lost the check.
    C. Take the necessary steps to have payment stopped on the check.
    D. Refrain from doing anything since the check may be found shortly.

19.____

20. A petty cash fund is set up PRIMARILY to

    A. take care of small investments that must be made from time to time
    B. take care of small expenses that arise from time to time
    C. provide a fund to be used as the office wants to use it with little need to maintain records
    D. take care of expenses that develop during emergencies such as machine breakdowns and fires

20.____

21. Your superior has asked you to send a package from your agency to a government agency in another city. He has written out the message and has indicated the name of the government agency.
When you prepare the package for mailing, which of the following items that your superior has not mentioned must you be sure to include?

21.____

A. Today's date
B. The full address of the government agency
C. A polite opening such as *Dear Sirs*
D. A final sentence such as *We would appreciate hearing from your agency in reply as soon as is convenient for you*

22. In addition to the original piece of correspondence, one should USUALLY also have typed

    22.____

  A. a single copy
  B. as many copies as can be typed at one time
  C. no more copies than are needed
  D. two copies

23. The one of the following which is the BEST procedure to follow when making a short insert in a completed dictation is to

    23.____

  A. label the insert with a letter and indicate the position of the insert in the text by writing the identifying letter in the proper place
  B. squeeze the insert into its proper place within the main text of the dictation
  C. take down the insert and check the placement with the person who dictated when you are ready to transcribe your notes
  D. transcribe the dictation into longhand, including the insert in its proper position

24. The one of the following procedures which will be MOST efficient in helping you to quickly open your dictation notebook to a clean sheet is to

    24.____

  A. clip or place a rubberband around the used portion of the notebook
  B. leave the book out and open to a clean page when not in use
  C. transcribe each dictation after it is given and rip out the used pages
  D. use a book marker to indicate which portion of the notebook has been used

25. The purpose of dating your dictation notebooks is GENERALLY to

    25.____

  A. enable you to easily refer to your notes at a later date
  B. ensure that you transcribe your notes in the order in which they were dictated
  C. set up a precise record-keeping procedure
  D. show your employer that you pay attention to detail

KEY (CORRECT ANSWERS)

1.	C	11.	A
2.	B	12.	B
3.	C	13.	D
4.	C	14.	D
5.	C	15.	C
6.	C	16.	D
7.	A	17.	B
8.	D	18.	C
9.	D	19.	C
10.	B	20.	B

21.	B
22.	C
23.	A
24.	A
25.	A

TEST 2

DIRECTIONS: Each question or incomplete statement is followed by several suggested answers or completions. Select the one that BEST answers the question or completes the statement. *PRINT THE LETTER OF THE CORRECT ANSWER IN THE SPACE AT THE RIGHT.*

1. With regard to typed correspondence received by most offices, which of the following is the GREATEST problem?   1.____

    A. Verbosity   B. Illegibility
    C. Improper folding   D. Excessive copies

2. Of the following, the GREATEST advantage of flash drives over rewritable CD storage is that they   2.____

    A. are portable
    B. are both smaller and lighter
    C. contain more storage space
    D. allow files to be deleted to free space

3. Suppose that a large quantity of information is in the files which are located a good distance from your desk. Almost every worker in your office must use these files constantly. Your duties in particular require that you daily refer to about 25 of the same items. They are short, one-page items distributed throughout the files. In this situation, your BEST course would be to   3.____

    A. take the items that you use daily from the files and keep them on your desk, inserting *out cards* in their place
    B. go to the files each time you need the information so that the items will be there when other workers need them
    C. make xerox copies of the information you use most frequently and keep them in your desk for ready reference
    D. label the items you use most often with different colored tabs for immediate identification

4. Of the following, the MOST important advantage of preparing manuals of office procedures in loose-leaf form is that this form   4.____

    A. permits several employees to use different sections simultaneously
    B. facilitates the addition of new material and the removal of obsolete material
    C. is more readily arranged in alphabetical order
    D. reduces the need for cross-references to locate material carried under several headings

5. Suppose that you establish a new clerical procedure for the unit you supervise. Your keeping a close check on the time required by your staff to handle the new procedure is WISE mainly because such a check will find out   5.____

    A. whether your subordinates know how to handle the new procedure
    B. whether a revision of the unit's work schedule will be necessary as a result of the new procedure
    C. what attitude your employees have toward the new procedure
    D. what alterations in job descriptions will be necessitated by the new procedure

6. The numbered statements below relate to the stenographic skill of taking dictation.   6.____
   According to authorities on secretarial practices, which of these are generally recommended guides to development of efficient stenographic skills?

STATEMENTS

1. A stenographer should date her notebook daily to facilitate locating certain notes
   at a later time.
2. A stenographer should make corrections of grammatical mistakes while her boss
   is dictating to her.
3. A stenographer should draw a line through the dictated matter in her notebook
   after she has transcribed it.
4. A stenographer should write in longhand unfamiliar names and addresses dictated to her.

The CORRECT answer is:

   A. Only Statements 1, 2, and 3 are generally recommended guides.
   B. Only Statements 2, 3, and 4 are generally recommended guides.
   C. Only Statements 1, 3, and 4 are generally recommended guides.
   D. All four statements are generally recommended guides.

7. According to generally recognized rules of filing in an alphabetic filing system, the one of   7.____
   the following names which normally should be filed LAST is

   A. Department of Education, New York State
   B. F.B.I.
   C. Police Department of New York City
   D. P.S. 81 of New York City

8. Which one of the following forms for the typed name of the dictator in the closing lines of   8.____
   a letter is generally MOST acceptable in the United States?

   A. (Dr.) James F. Fenton
   B. Dr. James F. Fenton
   C. Mr. James F. Fenton, Ph.D.
   D. James F. Fenton

9. Which of the following is, MOST generally, a rule to be followed when typing a rough   9.____
   draft?

   A. The copy should be single spaced.
   B. The copy should be triple spaced.
   C. There is no need for including footnotes.
   D. Errors must be neatly corrected.

10. An office assistant needs a synonym.   10.____
    Of the following, the book which she would find MOST useful is

    A. a world atlas
    B. BARTLETT'S FAMILIAR QUOTATIONS
    C. a manual of style
    D. a thesaurus

11. Of the following examples of footnotes, the one that is expressed in the MOST generally accepted standard form is: 11.____

   A. Johnson, T.F. (Dr.), <u>English for Everyone,</u> 3rd or 4th edition; New York City Linton Publishing Company, p. 467
   B. Frank Taylor, <u>English for Today</u> (New York: Rayton Publishing Company, 1971), p. 156
   C. Ralph Wilden,<u> English for Tomorrow,</u> Reynolds Publishing Company, England, p. 451
   D. Quinn, David, Yesterday's English (New York: Baldwin Publishing Company, 1972), p. 431

12. Standard procedures are used in offices PRIMARILY because   12.____

   A. an office is a happier place if everyone is doing the tasks in the same manner
   B. particular ways of doing jobs are considered more efficient than other ways
   C. it is good discipline for workers to follow standard procedures approved by the supervisor
   D. supervisors generally don't want workers to be creative in planning their work

13. Assume that an office assistant has the responsibility for compiling, typing, and mailing a preliminary announcement of Spring term course offerings. The announcement will go to approximately 900 currently enrolled students. Assuming that the following equipment is available for use, the MOST EFFECTIVE method for distributing the announcement to all 900 students is to   13.____

   A. e-mail it as a text document using the electronic student mailing list
   B. post the announcement as a PDF document for download on the department website
   C. send it by fax
   D. post the announcement and leave copies in buildings around campus

14. *Justified typing* is a term that refers MOST specifically to typewriting copy   14.____

   A. that has been edited and for which final copy is being prepared
   B. in a form that allows for an even right-hand margin
   C. with a predetermined vertical placement for each alternate line
   D. that has been approved by the supervisor and his superior

15. Which one of the following is the BEST form for the address in a letter?   15.____

   A. Mr. John Jones
      Vice President, The Universal Printing Company
      1220 Fifth Avenue
      New York, 10023 New York
   B. Mr. John Jones, Vice President
      The Universal Printing Company
      1220 Fifth Avenue
      New York, New York 10023
   C. Mr. John Jones, Vice President, The Universal Printing Company
      1220 Fifth Avenue
      New York, New York 10023

D. Mr. John Jones Vice President,
The Universal Printing Company
1220 Fifth Avenue
New York, 10023 New York

16. Of the following, the CHIEF advantage of the use of window envelopes over ordinary   16._____
envelopes is that window envelopes

A. eliminate the need for addressing envelopes
B. protect the confidential nature of enclosed material
C. cost less to buy than ordinary envelopes
D. reduce the danger of the address becoming illegible

17. In the complimentary close of a business letter, the FIRST letter of _____ should be   17._____
capitalized.

A. all the words   B. none of the words
C. only the first word   D. only the last word

18. Assume that one of your duties is to procure needed office supplies from the supply   18._____
room. You are permitted to draw supplies every two weeks.
The one of the following which would be the MOST desirable practice for you to follow
in obtaining supplies is to

A. obtain a quantity of supplies sufficient to last for several months to make certain
that enough supplies are always on hand
B. determine the minimum supply necessary to keep on hand for the various items and
obtain an additional quantity as soon as possible after the supply on hand has been
reduced to this minimum
C. review the supplies once a month to determine what items have been exhausted
and obtain an additional quantity as soon as possible
D. obtain a supply of an item as soon after it has been exhausted as is possible

19. Some offices that keep carbon copies of letters use several different colors of carbon   19._____
paper for making carbon copies.
Of the following, the CHIEF reason for using different colors of carbon paper is to

A. facilitate identification of different types of letters in the files
B. relieve the monotony of typing and filing carbon copies
C. reduce the costs of preparing carbon copies
D. utilize both sides of the carbon paper for typing

20. Your supervisor asks you to post an online ad for freelance designers interested in   20._____
submitting samples for a new company logo. Prospective workers should be proficient in
which of the following software?

A. Microsoft Word   B. Adobe Acrobat Pro
C. Adobe Illustrator   D. Microsoft PowerPoint

21. Gary Thompson is applying for a position with the firm of Gray and Williams.   21._____
Which letter should be filed in top position in the *Application* folder?

A. A letter of recommendation written on September 18 by Johnson & Smith
B. Williams' letter of October 8 requesting further details regarding Thompson's experience

C. Thompson's letter of September 8 making application for a position as sales manager
D. Letter of September 20 from Alfred Jackson recommending Thompson for the job

22. The USUAL arrangement in indexing the names of the First National Bank, Toledo, is   22.____

   A. First National Bank, Toledo, Ohio
   B. Ohio, First National Bank, Toledo
   C. Toledo, First National Bank, Ohio
   D. Ohio, Toledo, First National Bank

23. A single line through typed text indicating that it's incorrect or invalid is known as a(n)   23.____

   A. underline
   B. strikethrough
   C. line font
   D. eraser

24. A typical e-mail with an attachment should contain all of the following for successful   24.____
   transmittal EXCEPT

   A. recipient's address   B. file attachment
   C. body text   D. description of attachment

25. The subject line in a letter is USUALLY typed a _____ space below the _____.   25.____

   A. single; inside address   B. single; salutation
   C. double; inside address   D. double; salutation

KEY (CORRECT ANSWERS)

1.	A		11.	B
2.	C		12.	B
3.	C		13.	A
4.	B		14.	B
5.	B		15.	B
6.	C		16.	A
7.	D		17.	C
8.	D		18.	B
9.	B		19.	A
10.	D		20.	C

21.	B
22.	A
23.	B
24.	D
25.	D

EXAMINATION SECTION

TEST 1

DIRECTIONS: Each question or incomplete statement is followed by several suggested answers or completions. Select the one that BEST answers the question or completes the statement. *PRINT THE LETTER OF THE CORRECT ANSWER IN THE SPACE AT THE RIGHT.*

1. A DMV clerk is assisting a customer who is seeking to renew his driver's license. The customer becomes agitated and confrontational over how long it is taking. Which of the following would be the BEST response for a positive outcome in this situation?
   A. Tell the customer to leave and come back when he is in a better mood
   B. Attempt to de-escalate the situation while also efficiently completing the renewal
   C. Explain that policy does not allow the workers to move any faster
   D. See if another employee can take over while avoiding direct contact with the hostile customer

1.____

2. A village employee fields a call and question about an upcoming event at Town Hall for which he does not know the answer.
   Which is the BEST response for him to make?
   A. "Great question; let me find that out for you right now!"
   B. "Oh that is a good question...I don't know."
   C. "You need to call back later when a supervisor can answer your question."
   D. "What a good question! Unfortunately, I'm new here and don't know all of the policies. Let me see if I can look it up and I'll call you right back."

2.____

3. A customer walks into the post office and wants to buy the new limited-edition collectible stamps, but they were not shipped on time so the postal clerk will not have them for another few days.
   What should the clerk do to remedy this situation?
   A. Tell the customer the stamps are back-ordered and unavailable at this time
   B. Apologize and offer to give the customer the phone number to another post office to see if they have the stamps
   C. Apologize for the delay and give the customer the specific date that the stamps will be available
   D. Tell the customer the post office operates on a first come, first serve basis and she'll have to check back each day if she wants to make sure they received the stamps

3.____

4. A translator for the Department of Justice receives a call from someone seeking information about one of his family members, but is unable to fully meet the needs of the caller because of the translator's unfamiliarity with the speaker's dialect.

4.____

How should the translator handle this situation?
- A. "Sir, I am sorry but I'm going to have to transfer you to someone else."
- B. "Hi, sorry to interrupt, but you will need to call back with someone who can speak a little more clearly."
- C. "Hello, I am sorry, but I am having trouble understanding you. Would you mind if I transfer you to someone else?"
- D. "Hello, Mr. [Last Name]! Let's get this problem resolved for you. I'm going to transfer you to a senior linguist that specializes in your specific dialect. They will be able to best aid you."

5. A doctor for the Department of Veterans Affairs is working with a patient who asks her to prescribe some extra medication to help with his pain. The doctor has already given him the appropriate amount.
What should the doctor do?
- A. Explain that as much as she'd like to fulfill the patient's request, the medication policy in place is too important as it deals with the patient's safety and health
- B. Ignore the request and pretend as though she didn't hear the patient
- C. Give the patient the medication if he obviously needs it for pain management
- D. Report the patient to the police and have him arrested for attempting to possess controlled substances

5.____

6. A local resident comes into Village Hall upset because someone issued him the wrong permit for a deck renovation on his house.
As someone who did NOT issue the permit, how should the employee handle this situation?
- A. Ask the resident to show proof of the wrong permit and then ask what permit he should have
- B. Explain to the resident that it could not have been the fault of the Village Hall employee and that he [the resident] must have submitted the wrong application
- C. Tell the resident how sorry he is that this happened, attempt to explain what could have happened and then resolve the situation by approving the correct permit
- D. Find out who sold him the wrong permit and explain that the employee was wrong, and then find the employee and have them fix their mistake

6.____

7. A local park district that recently joined Twitter has received public backlash from its residents due to poor communication. In one specific instance, a children's art class was canceled, but the park district did not announce it until after the event would have started.
How should the person in charge of the Twitter account respond to angry residents who have complained about the lack of communication?
- A. Tell them to contact the park district anytime between 9 A.M. and 5 P.M. which are the normal operating hours
- B. Post a silly meme that makes fun of the park district's slow response and also acts as an apology

7.____

C. Put out a message that apologizes for tardiness, assures better communication and offers a discount on other programs
D. Tweet out an offer of a partial refund (for the missed class), a sincere apology, and a promise to communicate better going forward

8. A postal employee overhears a customer at the post office make the following statement to a co-worker who has Chinese ancestry: "Are you Shu? Or Mou? I can never tell you guys apart!" The customer seems jovial and not angry, but it is clear the co-worker is bothered by this interaction.
What should the employee do?
   A. Yell at the customer and tell him to come back when he is not so racist
   B. Take over for the co-worker and explain to the customer that she would be glad to help, but only on the basis of mutual respect
   C. Attempt to explain to the customer that his joke is prejudiced and unacceptable
   D. Ignore the situation and try to comfort the co-worker after the customer has left

8.____

9. A female Village Hall clerk has been working with a resident all day and has built up a rapport with him while assisting with his issue. As their business starts to conclude, the resident asks if the clerk would like to grab a bite to eat or some coffee after they're done for the day. The clerk is uncomfortable and unsure of what to do.
How should she respond?
   A. "Oh, I'm so tired and I think someone else can handle the rest of your business today."
   B. "That is thoughtful of you, but I'd like to keep this professional and focus on finishing up our business here."
   C. "I suppose we could grab a small bite to eat before I head home."
   D. "Please do not ask me out on a date! You are completely out of line!"

9.____

10. A participant in one of the town-run youth leagues broke his arm two days before the league was set to kick off. Because of the injury, he will be unable to participate, so the boy's mother asks the youth league director for a refund. The mother signed a waiver that clearly states that no refunds can be issued for the league within a week of it starting. Despite this, she asks for an exception because of the circumstance.
What should the league director do?
   A. Attempt to explain why the policy is the way it is, show he understands the frustration of the parent, but there is nothing that can be done
   B. Empathize with the parent and show agreement with her, but explain that is not something that can be changed by one person and promise to take this to a superior to solve the issue.
   C. Make it clear that an alternative to the policy will be sought, offer another league or activity that the boy could be a part of, or waive the cost of the league for the next year.
   D. Explain that the boy and parent should have been more aware of activities that might cause injury and share educational materials on injury prevention and rehabilitation.

10.____

11. An employee that works for the state's tourism department receives a phone call from a potential tourist asking for information about attractions. As he starts to answer, the caller interrupts, asks inappropriate questions, and seems to be trying to frustrate the employee.
How should this situation be handled?

    A. He should play it cool by explaining that they would love to answer any actual questions if the caller is being sincere, and if insincere, explain that he needs to attend to other callers who have legitimate questions
    B. He should stay civil and answer all questions the caller has
    C. He should become aggressive and rude back to the caller before hanging up
    D. He should tell the caller he will be right back, but leave the caller on hold indefinitely

11.____

12. An employee in the Citizen Service and Response Department for a town in Virginia handles non-emergency citizen service requests. Recently, the employee received praise via Twitter for an expedient solution to a child's need, but the employee was not the one who actually solved the citizen's problem.
What should she do?

    A. Denounce the tweet as false and tweet about the person who deserves the praise
    B. Take credit for the tweet, but be sure to mention others that were involved
    C. Reach out to the citizen outside of social media and explain who the real hero was
    D. Express gratitude for the recognition, but highlight the coworker who was truly responsible

12.____

13. A resident complains to you that your facility is making exaggerated and false claims about the benefits of joining their exercise classes. She wants you to immediately take down the advertisement and publicly apologize for misleading the community.
What should you do?

    A. Refer her to your supervisor – this is well above your pay grade
    B. Act like you are interested, but dismiss the resident's claim as crazy and does not warrant taking action
    C. Listen with an open mind, and determine if there is any truth to the resident's claims. Make a promise to look into the matter, but do not commit to changing anything
    D. Immediately take down the advertisement and issue the apology. Residents' tax dollars are responsible for the funding you receive, so you cannot risk angering them

13.____

14. A customer becomes confused as to which line he is supposed to be on
at the DMV. After a lengthy wait, the man arrives at your station for a license
renewal, but you explain you are working on license-plate renewals only. He
slumps his shoulders and displays some distress before imploring you to make
an exception for him so he does not have to go back to the end of the line and
start all over.
   What should you do?
   A. Tell him you would love to help, but do not have the required equipment
      to complete his request
   B. Garner the attention of your co-worker who is working license renewal
      and have him put the customer higher up in his queue
   C. Repeat your initial statement that he is in the wrong line, then ignore his
      request and ask for the next customer in line
   D. Leave your post and have the customer follow. Explain the situation to
      your co-worker working at license renewal and have the customer jump to
      the front of the line

14.____

15. A Village Hall employee is talking on the phone with a resident who needs help
registering for a program electronically, but during the discussion the employee
realizes the resident is not at home and does not have access to necessary
registration information.
   How should the employee proceed?
   A. Direct the customer to look for the answer on the village's website when
      she is at home
   B. Hang up on the caller – obviously, she does not know what she is doing
      and does not deserve the help
   C. Tell the customer that she cannot be helped until she has the correct
      information, then politely end the call
   D. Establish a time for the person to call back when she is able to provide
      the relevant information

15.____

16. An employee at the Recreational Center receives a phone call from a
resident who says, "I am very upset that my meeting with your service director
did not start at the appointed time. I was told the meeting would start at 11:30
A.M. and he did not arrive until 12:15 P.M. I took the morning off from work to
make this meeting, but I did not need to if I had known the meeting was going
to be so late!" After politely putting the person on hold, the employee calls the
director who tells her the meeting began late because of heavy traffic and a
previous meeting that had run long.
   Once the employee takes the resident off hold, how should she respond?
   A. Offer sincere apologies and explain what happened without making
      excuses for the late start to the meeting
   B. Apologize profusely to the resident, but give the contact information for
      the director, so the director can explain what happened
   C. Tell the resident that sometimes meetings run late and that she could
      have left if she wanted to, as it was a voluntary meeting
   D. Ask the resident what she would like the employee to do about the
      situation

16.____

23

17. An elderly customer calls the post office with a problem finding some product information on the website. He is polite yet frustrated and upset that he cannot find the information he is seeking. The post office employee recognizes what the elderly man is looking for, but realizes the information is too long and complicated to share over the phone.
    What are the BEST steps for the employee to take?
    A. Tell him he can find the information he is looking for in the product information section of the website
    B. Offer to find the specific information he needs and send it to him directly
    C. Advise him to go to the product information section of the website and print out all of the available material so that he can review it offline
    D. Help him navigate the website to find the information he is looking for

    17.____

18. A DMV clerk is attempting to explain procedures to a customer that seems to be hard of hearing. The clerk explains twice, but the customer does not seem to understand.
    What should the clerk do?
    A. Explain that he is not sure what the customer does not understand and walk away
    B. Ask someone else to help the customer
    C. Repeat the procedures for the third time and try to explain it slightly differently
    D. Repeat the procedures for the third time and then ask for the next customer in line

    18.____

19. A resident is considering signing up for a fitness program through the park district, though the trainer running the program knows it will not completely fulfill the customer's needs.
    What should the trainer do?
    A. Alert the resident to what the program will actually cover and explain that it is still worth the customer's time even if it doesn't fully meet what he is looking for
    B. Answer any questions the customer may have, but do nothing else, as the trainer can support the customer after they've started
    C. Suggest that a non-district fitness program might be better and offer to find the information for him
    D. Make any promises and guarantees about the program that is needed. Once he signs up, the customer is not the employee's concern anymore

    19.____

20. A resident comes into a county clerk's office looking upset and distraught.
    How can the clerk display active listening skills so the resident can at least know that her voice was heard?
    A. Nod along with the resident's story the entire time
    B. Frequently interrupt to see if the resident needs any water or snacks while she tells her story
    C. Use phrases like "I see" or "Go on" whenever it seems to be an appropriate pause
    D. Both A and C

    20.____

21. A public defense attorney meets with a client who becomes aggressive and combative when the attorney asks for clarification on an event that the client was a part of.
    How should the attorney respond?
    A. Change his behavior in various ways to get the best possible outcome
    B. Mirror the client's behavior, becoming frustrated and aggressive
    C. Walk out of the meeting. If the client will not respect the attorney, then why should the attorney respect the client?
    D. None of the above

21.____

22. A very important resident of your village contacts your department and is upset about the way one of your co-workers handled the processing of his permit application.
    Which of the following is the BEST way to move forward with this situation?
    A. Rush to respond to him right away as he is very important and busy
    B. Take responsibility for the mix-up and attempt to figure out how to appropriately fix the issue
    C. Attempt to see why he is so antagonistic and suggest he is part of the problem
    D. Make promises about fixing the issue as promptly as possible, even if you cannot actually keep the promise

22.____

23. An administrative assistant for the local police station receives a phone call from an angry resident. The assistant wants to aid in resolving the resident's issue and calm her down before she talks to an officer.
    Which of the following steps should the assistant take while talking to the resident?
    A. Empathize   B. Diagnose
    C. Apologize   D. All of the above

23.____

24. After an ice storm passed through the area, the steps outside of Village Hall iced over. While an employee attempted to salt the area outside the building, a person slipped and fell as they were attempting to come in for a meeting.
    How should this situation be handled?
    A. Start gathering evidence to prove that reasonable attempts were made to prevent injury for customers walking into the building
    B. Call insurance to get a claims adjustor out to the building as fast as possible to assist the person
    C. Get immediate medical attention for the person who is injured
    D. None of the above

24.____

25. A local customer of the park district tweets in their Twitter account poking fun at how slow and behind the times the park district is. After a week, the comments do not seem to stop.
Which of the following should the park district NOT do regarding the customer and their tweets?
    A. Directly contact the Twitter user to see what ways the park district could improve their slow process
    B. Before responding, check to ensure the response is professional and courteous
    C. Censor the Twitter account responsible for the tweet
    D. The park district should avoid doing all of the things mentioned above

25.____

KEY (CORRECT ANSWERS)

1.	B		11.	A
2.	A		12.	D
3.	C		13.	C
4.	D		14.	B
5.	A		15.	D
6.	C		16.	A
7.	D		17.	B
8.	B		18.	C
9.	B		19.	A
10.	C		20.	D

21.	A
22.	B
23.	D
24.	C
25.	C

TEST 2

DIRECTIONS: Each question or incomplete statement is followed by several suggested answers or completions. Select the one that BEST answers the question or completes the statement. *PRINT THE LETTER OF THE CORRECT ANSWER IN THE SPACE AT THE RIGHT.*

1.   Recently, the village mayor made controversial statements that angered many of the local residents. An employee at Village Hall has received a call from one of these angry people.
How should she handle this situation?
A. Deny any knowledge of the situation and explain that it is not her job to comment on the mayor's opinions
B. Apologize and be transparent about what happened
C. Give the person the mayor's phone number at Village Hall and explain they should be talking to the mayor
D. Once the employee realizes what the phone call is about, she should see if there is any constructive criticism to bring to the mayor and promise to do so

1.____

2.   A local patron comes into the library and claims that he was charged for not returning a book that he says was returned to the drop box after the library was closed. The librarian knows that the patron never returned the book and is just trying to avoid paying the fine for a lost book.
Which of the following statements should she make to the patron?
A. "Sir, I know you're frustrated and I completely empathize. My goal is to help you sort this out."
B. "Listen, I know you lost the book and you know you lost the book, so let's stop playing games and you can pay your fine if you wish to continue to check out books here."
C. "Sir, I am so sorry that this happened! I know we'll get to the bottom of this and that starts with everyone's being honest."
D. "Sir, I tell you what. Do not worry about it. I am sure the book was returned and we just misplaced it. I'll wipe the fine and you can go ahead and check out any books you wish."

2.____

3.   A resident calls the park district fitness center to cancel her membership.
What should the employee who receives the call do?
A. Attempt to convince the resident to keep her membership by promoting the health benefits of an active lifestyle
B. Keep the resident on the line and attempt to have her join another activity such as a league or tennis lessons
C. Apologize that the fitness center could not fit her needs, cancel the membership, and ask what went wrong so the center can improve in the future.
D. Cancel the membership and promptly hang up

3.____

4. The local post office receives a phone call from an angry customer who wants   4.____
   to know why her package has not yet arrived. Upon checking the tracking for
   the package, the employee cannot determine where the package is.
   How should he proceed?
   A. Apologize for the package not arriving on time
   B. Admit that as of right now the package cannot be located
   C. Explain the process for filing a claim on a missing or lost package
   D. All of the above

5. An IRS employee recently received training on how to comply with equality   5.____
   legislation when a customer calls asking for assistance on a tax issue they're
   having.
   How should this recent training affect that phone call?
   A. Range of services will decrease   B. Service offer will be limited
   C. Fair service will be provided   D. Range of services will increase

6. A customer attempts to reach out to the Public Works Department of her   6.____
   local government via Twitter to ask a question about garbage collection. The
   Public Works main Twitter account informs the customer that she will need to
   contact the Garbage Collection Twitter account in order for her question to be
   answered. The customer is frustrated because of how long it is taking for her
   to receive a simple answer.
   How could Public Works improve in the future to improve its social media
   customer service?
   A. Assess the need for multiple accounts for the department, as it could be
      better to have one social media platform with shared ownership between
      departments.
   B. Educate each department's social media team on how to provide the best
      possible customer care via social media.
   C. Ask customers to contact the department by more conventional means in
      order to better handle customer service
   D. Both A and B

7. An irate resident telephones a clerk who handles housing tax assessment for the   7.____
   town.
   How should the clerk react so that the customer's expectations are met with a
   positive outcome?
   A. Follow the department's procedures for this kind of call
   B. Describe why the issue happened
   C. Explain that there are new members on staff
   D. Support the department's position and not the resident

8. A concerned citizen is following up on a report she made to Child and Youth   8.____
   Services two days ago.
   What should the employee receiving the citizen's follow-up do to make sure the
   situation is handled effectively?

    A. Issue the full report to the citizen
    B. Express gratitude for filing a report and explain that Child and Youth Services takes it very seriously and is looking into the matter. Tell her "No comment" and that it is the policy of Child and Youth Services to not discuss open or closed investigations with citizens
    C. Explain to the citizen that the report has been filed and the situation has been taken care of
    D. None of the above

9. When a customer asks why Village Hall needs him to fill out an online survey he just received, what should the employee's explanation be?   9.____
    A. So organizational procedure changes can be avoided
    B. So changes can be made to ensure and maintain customer loyalty
    C. So customers can be added to an e-mail list that informs of upcoming events
    D. So information can be gathered and shared with other organizations and departments

10. Someone walks into the local Health Department looking to talk to anyone who works there. The employee who helps her has no knowledge of the person or the meeting ahead of time.   10.____
What question should the employee ask to help establish the person's needs?
    A. "Are you happy with how you've been treated so far?"
    B. "Would you be willing to fill out a survey after this to attest to the great care and service you received today?"
    C. "I would love to help you, but I do not know what you need yet."
    D. "Is there anything I can help you with today?"

11. A teenager who recently passed her driving test seems very nervous when she approaches the DMV employee who will process her request.   11.____
What technique can the employee use to help put the teen at ease?
    A. Ask the teen to hurry up
    B. Avoid speaking to the teen beyond what is necessary to process her request as quickly and efficiently as possible
    C. Relate to the teen by reminiscing about the employee's own experience
    D. Have a younger, friendlier-looking co-worker help the teen. It may put her at ease if she is closer in age.

12. During a customer interaction at the post office, an employee asks for the customer's e-mail address. The customer wants to know why they need an e-mail address.   12.____
The employee explains that he needs the e-mail address because
    A. it will help with business analysis by seeing what kind of customers the office receives
    B. it will help increase customer loyalty through deal alerts and promotional activities
    C. it allows the post office to gain more information on its customers which it shares with the federal government
    D. all of the above

13. A man comes into the state tollway office and asks to talk to a specific employee. When he meets the employee, the person is upset because he claims the employee promised to waive fees attached to his account, but the person just received a final notice that those fees needed to be paid or further action would be taken.
Knowing that he did make the promise, what should the employee do?
    A. Explain that the promise he made was overruled by his supervisor and that the customer must pay the fines
    B. Pretend like no promise was ever offered and tell the person he'll have to pay the fee
    C. Waive the fee and live with any potential consequences of disappointing management. A promise is a promise.
    D. None of the above

13.____

14. A public service employee is meeting with a local customer who is upset with how his claim has been handled.
Which of the following should the employee AVOID doing if he wants the meeting to go well?
    A. Listen to the complaint and show empathy
    B. Take an important text/phone call during the meeting
    C. Tell the customer he will fix this issue together and solicit ideas from the customer about what he would be satisfied with
    D. Let the customer know that the employee will do everything possible to help the customer with what he needs

14.____

15. A woman walks into the post office with a damaged package she claims she received yesterday.
Which of the following should the employee NOT state to the woman during the ensuing conversation?
    A. "I am so sorry your product arrived damaged!"
    B. "I see your package was insured; would you like my assistance in filing an indemnity claim?"
    C. "I have had this happen to me before as well. I know how frustrated you are right now!"
    D. "I will contact your business and reorder that item for you."

15.____

16. The university bookstore receives a complaint from a customer who claims she bought an item there yesterday and then found it went on clearance today.
What should the employee who received the customer do?
    A. Ask for the customer's item and receipt to confirm the purchase date, then credit the difference back to the customer
    B. Explain that the customer can return the item, but cannot repurchase it in order to get the discount
    C. Speak with management to ensure a credit can be given and then give it to the customer
    D. Apologize for the frustration, but explain that policy does not allow for any returns or exchanges on clearance items

16.____

17. A dissatisfied resident engages Village Hall via Twitter to complain about the lack of quality in the road maintenance outside her house after a winter storm. How should the person in charge of social media respond to the resident's tweet?
    She should
    A. not respond, as Village Hall cannot fix every small problem and trying to respond will only call more attention to the issue.
    B. tweet back for the resident to call Village Hall during normal operating hours in order to discuss the issue
    C. directly message the resident to find out why she was dissatisfied and attempt to garner feedback about a better process for fixing the issue
    D. mention the company that is contracted to handle road maintenance, so they can take care of the problem

17.____

18. An employee who is responsible for social media posts for the Parks and Recreation Department notices that a number of negative reviews recently posted about the department all seem to be made by the same online profile. After digging around, the employee determines that the profile belongs to someone who recently had a bad experience with one of the programs run by the department.
    What should the employee do?
    A. Call out the person by showing that their bad reviews are based off one experience
    B. Post a general statement about how the Parks and Recreation Department values all customers/residents and strives to give them the best possible experience
    C. Ignore the comments and trust the public to know that one person posting negative reviews does not mean the department has a negative reputation
    D. Seek out the person privately and attempt to correct any wrongdoing on the part of the department

18.____

19. An employee for City Hall must meet with a group of concerned citizens for input on a potential City park project.
    How should the employee dress for this meeting?
    A. Dress casually because the meeting might take long
    B. Dress professionally to convey competence and ability to meet the citizens' needs
    C. Dress casually to put the citizens at ease during the meeting
    D. Dress professionally to intimidate the citizens and show superiority

19.____

20. A customer comes into the State Tollway Office and complains that he was given a defective sensor for electronic payment of tolls.
    Which of the following should the employee NOT do in his attempt to help resolve this situation?
    A. Give the customer personal contact information so he can contact the employee anytime there is an issue in the future
    B. Reimburse the customer with a new sensor

20.____

C. Compensate the customer by waiving any extra fees that may have incurred from the unprocessed tolls
D. Offer the customer a sincere apology for the inconvenience he's had to endure

21. A customer places a complicated order over the telephone.
What is the BEST way to ensure the details of the order are correct?
   A. Repeat the order over the telephone
   B. Record the telephone call
   C. Confirm the order in writing
   D. Take down the details in writing

21.____

22. There is a new initiative from Village Hall to promote a healthier lifestyle for residents and part of the program launch features employees calling residents and then scheduling meetings to explain the initiative in greater detail. When one employee meets with a resident, the resident interrupts their original pitch and asks simply why they need to hear about the features and benefits of the program.
How should the employee respond?
   A. Kindly ask the resident to stop interrupting so he can explain everything
   B. Let the resident know that is how they will understand what the program will do for them
   C. Explain that is how residents will understand the details of the program
   D. Both B and C

22.____

23. A customer telephones the County Clerk's office complaining that her ADA rights are being violated because the handicapped parking space is not wide enough to accommodate her and her vehicle. The employee speaking to the customer knows that the parking space is the required 96 inches wide, but also knows that the size of a parking lot sometimes makes it difficult for customers to park correctly.
How should the employee handle this situation?
   A. Apologize to the customer and politely end the conversation. Then call the lawyer that represents the County for legal representation and counsel.
   B. Express empathy that the clerk's office is such a hassle for the customer, but explain that the building is ADA compliant. Offer to collaborate on a solution that will work for the customer.
   C. Call the customer out for being wrong. Offer to show her any forms of plans that show that the clerk's office is ADA compliant.
   D. Explain to the customer that she is right and the clerk's office will attempt to make their parking lot and handicapped spaces more compliant for the customer.

23.____

24. A resident walks into the Homeowners' Association office and asks for the
deadline to file an application to run for one of the offices of the HOA. The
employee working does not know the answer.
What is the BEST way to respond to the resident's request?
    A. Tell the resident what she thinks the answer might be
    B. Refer the resident to a supervisor
    C. Inform the person that she does not know, but will find out as quickly as
    possible
    D. Explain that this kind of information is not something that can be given out
    to the public

24.____

25. A customer at the DMV asks an employee to do something that the employee
cannot accommodate.
In responding to the request, the employee should AVOID doing which of the
following?
    A. Quote DMV policy regarding the customer's request
    B. Explain to the customer why the employee cannot accommodate her
    request
    C. Make vague statements that allow for interpretation and, therefore, wiggle
    room
    D. Both A and C

25.____

KEY (CORRECT ANSWERS)

1.	B		11.	C
2.	A		12.	A
3.	C		13.	C
4.	D		14.	B
5.	C		15.	D
6.	D		16.	A
7.	A		17.	C
8.	B		18.	D
9.	B		19.	B
10.	D		20.	A

21.	A
22.	D
23.	B
24.	C
25.	D

EXAMINATION SECTION
TEST 1

DIRECTIONS: Each question or incomplete statement is followed by several suggested answers or completions. Select the one that BEST answers the question or completes the statement. *PRINT THE LETTER OF THE CORRECT ANSWER IN THE SPACE AT THE RIGHT.*

1. The detection of counterfeiting and the apprehension of counterfeiters Is PRIMARILY the responsibility of the   1.____

    A. Federal Bureau of Investigation
    B. United States Secret Service
    C. Federal Reserve Board
    D. National Security Council

2. The term *legal tender* applies to   2.____

    A. a check, legally endorsed, and intended for deposit only
    B. money which may lawfully be used in the payment of debts
    C. foreign money whose rate of exchange is set by law
    D. uncoined gold or silver in the form of bullion bars

Questions 3-4.

DIRECTIONS: Questions 3 and 4 are to be answered SOLELY on the basis of the information contained in the following statement:

When a design for a new bank note of the Federal Government has been prepared by the Bureau of Engraving and Printing and has been approved by the Secretary of the Treasury, the engravers begin the work of cutting the design in steel. No one engraver does all the work. Each man is a specialist. One works only on portraits, another on lettering, another on scroll work, and so on. Each engraver, with a steel tool known as a graver, and aided by a powerful magnifying glass, carefully carves his portion of the design into the steel. He knows that one false cut or a slip of his tool, or one miscalculation of width or depth of line, may destroy the merit of his work. A single mistake means that months or weeks of labor will have been in vain. The Bureau is proud of the fact that no counterfeiter ever has duplicated the excellent work of its expert engravers.

3. According to the above statement, each engraver in the Bureau of Engraving and Printing   3.____

    A. must be approved by the Secretary of the Treasury before he can begin work on the design for a new bank note
    B. is responsible for engraving a complete design of a new bank note himself
    C. designs new bank notes and submits them for approval to the Secretary of the Treasury
    D. performs only a specific part of the work of engraving a design for a new bank note

4. According to the above statement,   4.____

A. an engraver's tools are not available to a counterfeiter
B. mistakes made in engraving a design can be corrected immediately with little delay in the work of the Bureau
C. the skilled work of the engravers has not been successfully reproduced by counterfeiters
D. careful carving and cutting by the engravers is essential to prevent damage to equipment

5. The public lays down the rules governing the type of service that it expects to be given. These rules are expressed partly in laws and partly in public opinion, which at any time may be made into law. Private business and government departments have, and always have had, the task of giving the public what it expects, a task which has lately come to be called public relations. According to the above statement,   5.___

   A. government departments have the task of serving the public as it wishes to be served
   B. private firms emphasize public relations more than public agencies do
   C. the rules for giving the public the service it expects are all eventually made into laws
   D. the task of public relations is to inform the public about the work of government departments

6. Certain personal qualities are required of an employee who is to perform a particular assignment efficiently. Since each employee possesses different qualities, experience indicates that it is important to seek and select the employee who possesses the personal qualities required for the particular assignment.   6.___
   According to the above statement,

   A. the personal qualities of an employee should be changed to fit a particular assignment
   B. personal qualities are more important than experience in the performance of an assignment
   C. an assignment should be changed to fit the personal qualities of the employee assigned to it
   D. the employee selected for an assignment should have the personal qualities needed to perform it

7. A cashier has to make many arithmetic calculations in connection with his work. Skill in arithmetic comes readily with practice; no special talent is needed.   7.___
   On the basis of the above statement, it is MOST accurate to state that

   A. the most important part of a cashier's job is to make calculations
   B. few cashiers have the special ability needed to handle arithmetic problems easily
   C. without special talent, cashiers cannot learn to do the calculations they are required to do in their work
   D. a cashier can, with practice, learn to handle the computations he is required to make

8. A bonded employee is much less likely to be tempted to steal money than an unbonded   8.____
one, for he knows that a bonding company will prosecute him for the sake of principle,
whereas an employer might not ordinarily take any action against an employee if there is
no hope of recovering the stolen money.
The MOST valid implication of the above statement is that

    A.   a bonded employee if often tempted to steal because he knows that his employer
is protected against the loss
    B.   a bonding company will attempt to find and punish the guilty employee even when
the stolen money cannot be recovered
    C.   an employer whose bonded employees do not steal is wasting the money spent to
bond them
    D.   it is wasteful for a bonding company to prosecute an employee when there is no
chance of recovering the stolen money

9. The BEST of the following attitudes regarding departmental rules and regulations for a   9.____
cashier to take is that they

    A.   are simply a means for justifying disciplinary action taken by a supervisor
    B.   are to be interpreted by each employee as he sees fit
    C.   must be obeyed even if they seem unreasonable in some cases
    D.   should be read and studied but may be ignored whenever an employee feels it is
necessary to do so

10. It is MOST important for a cashier who is assigned to perform a lengthy monotonous task   10.____
to

    A.   perform this task before doing his other work
    B.   ask another cashier to assist him to dispose of the task quickly
    C.   perform this task only when his other work has been completed
    D.   take measures to prevent mistakes in performing this task

11. Although accuracy and speed are both important for a cashier in the performance of his   11.____
work, accuracy should be considered more important MAINLY because

    A.   most supervisors insist on accurate work
    B.   much time is lost in correcting errors
    C.   a rapid rate of work cannot be maintained for any length of time
    D.   speedy workers are usually inaccurate

12. Of the following, the CHIEF reason why a cashier should not be late to work in the morn-   12.____
ing is that

    A.   he will probably be penalized for his lateness
    B.   the work of his unit may be delayed because of his tardiness
    C.   he will set a bad example for the other employees to follow
    D.   a poor attendance record may affect his supervisor's evaluation of his work

13. A cashier who handles large quantities of currency should know that the term *Silver Cer-*   13.____
tificate usually referred to

    A.   a receipt for silver bars deposited with a bank
    B.   a form of paper money that is acceptable only for the payment of non-business
debts

C. a certificate issued by a refiner of silver metal to show the purity of his product
D. a form of paper money that is backed by silver owned by the United States Government

14. There are 12 consecutively numbered Federal Reserve Districts, each having as its symbol a number and the corresponding letter of the alphabet. The Federal Reserve Bank in each district has the same symbol as that of its district. For example, the Federal Reserve Bank of Boston is in the first Federal Reserve District and has as its symbol the number *1* and the letter *A*. The other districts, in numerical order, are New York, Philadelphia, Cleveland, Richmond, Atlanta, Chicago, St. Louis, Minneapolis, Kansas City, Dallas, and San Francisco.
According to the above statement, the Federal Reserve Bank of Philadelphia is represented by the

14.____

A. number *2* and the letter *B*
B. number *2* and the letter *C*
C. number *3* and the letter *B*
D. number *3* and the letter *C*

15. Of the following, the MOST important reason for a cashier to know the portraits that appear on each denomination of paper currency is that

15.____

A. he will be able to count bills merely by looking at the portraits
B. familiarity with portraits may help him to identify a counterfeit bill that has had its denomination changed from a lower to a higher amount
C. a greater knowledge of currency may help increase his promotional opportunities
D. the United States Treasury Department sometimes changes the portraits appearing on various currency denominations

16. The one of the following which is a characteristic of a genuine bill is that its portrait

16.____

A. has a fine screen of regular lines in its background
B. has irregular and broken lines in its background
C. has a very dark blue background
D. merges into the background

17. Of the following characteristics, the one that is LEAST helpful in deciding whether a bill is counterfeit is that the

17.____

A. portrait is dull, smudgy or scratchy
B. serial numbers are unevenly spaced
C. geometric lathework is broken and indistinct
D. ink rubs off when the bill is rubbed on a piece of paper

18. The color of the Treasury seal and serial number on a United States Note is always

18.____

A. blue   B. gray   C. green   D. red

19. The saw teeth points on the rim of the Treasury seal on a genuine bill are generally

19.____

A. blunt and uneven   B. broken off and faded
C. indistinct   D. sharp and evenly spaced

20. If one-half of a mutilated genuine bill is sent to the Currency Redemption Division of the Treasury Department, the bill will

    A.   be redeemed at one-half of its face value
    B.   be redeemed at three-fifths of its face value
    C.   be redeemed at its full face value
    D.   not be redeemed at all

20.____

21. The color of the Treasury seal and serial number on a Federal Reserve Note is always

    A.   blue   B.   brown   C.   green   D.   red

21.____

22. The serial number on the face of a bill is printed

    A.   to the right of the portrait and to the lower left of the portrait
    B.   to the left of the portrait and to the lower right of the portrait
    C.   directly above the portrait and directly below the portrait
    D.   in the upper left corner and the lower left corner

22.____

23. The color of the check letter on the face of a bill is always

    A.   black   B.   blue   C.   green   D.   red

23.____

24. The face plate number on the face of a bill is printed in the

    A.   upper left corner   B.   upper right corner
    C.   lower left corner   D.   lower right corner

24.____

25. If three-fifths of a mutilated genuine bill is sent to the Currency Redemption Division of the Treasury Department, the bill will

    A.   be redeemed at one-half of its face value
    B.   be redeemed at three-fifths of its face value
    C.   be redeemed at its full face value
    D.   not be redeemed at all

25.____

Questions 26 - 35.

DIRECTIONS: In Column I below are listed the names of ten men and buildings. In Column II are listed seven paper currency denominations and a category *None of the above denominations.*

                In questions 26 to 35, for each man or building in Column I, print in the correspondingly numbered space on your answer sheet, the capital letter preceding the denomination in Column II on which the man or building appears. If the man or building appears on none of the listed denominations, print the letter *H* in the correspondingly numbered space on your answer sheet.

COLUMN I		COLUMN II		
26.	Alexander Hamilton	A.	$1	26.__
27.	White House	B.	$2	27.__
28.	Benjamin Franklin	C.	$5	28.__
29.	Mount Vernon	D.	$10	29.__
30.	Thomas Jefferson	E.	$20	30.__
31.	U.S. Treasury Department	F.	$50	31.__
32.	Andrew Jackson	G.	$100	32.__
33.	United States Capitol	H.	None of the above denominations	33.__
34.	George Washington			34.__
35.	Abraham Lincoln			35.__

KEY (CORRECT ANSWERS)

1.	B	11.	B	21.	C	31.	D
2.	B	12.	B	22.	A	32.	E
3.	D	13.	D	23.	A	33.	F
4.	C	14.	D	24.	D	34.	A
5.	A	15.	B	25.	C	35.	C
6.	D	16.	A	26.	D		
7.	D	17.	D	27.	E		
8.	B	18.	D	28.	G		
9.	C	19.	D	29.	H		
10.	D	20.	A	30.	B		

TEST 2

DIRECTIONS: Each question or incomplete statement is followed by several suggested answers or completions. Select the one that BEST answers the question or completes the statement. *PRINT THE LETTER OF THE CORRECT ANSWER IN THE SPACE AT THE RIGHT.*

1. Of the following, the characteristic which describes a genuine coin MOST accurately is that the coin usually

    A. can be bent easily at the edges
    B. can be cut easily with a knife
    C. has a bell-like ring when dropped on a hard surface
    D. will not bounce when dropped on a hard surface

1.____

2. The corrugations on the outer edge of a genuine coin are usually

    A. even and regular
    B. indistinct and blackened
    C. the same as on a counterfeit coin
    D. uneven and crooked

2.____

3. When comparing counterfeit coins with genuine ones, most counterfeit coins usually feel

    A. greasy   B. cold   C. sticky   D. damp

3.____

4. A cashier who, in the course of his duties, suffers even a minor cut should have it properly cared for so that there will be no chance for infection to set in. Amputations, and even deaths, have resulted from small neglected wounds. According to the above statement, it is MOST accurate to state that

    A. a minor cut is not usually a cause for concern
    B. minor injuries are usually worse than they seem to be
    C. minor injuries should not be neglected
    D. small wounds are more dangerous than big ones

4.____

5. Certain types of money may be photographed only with the permission of the Secretary of the Treasury. His permission is not required to photograph

    A. bills   B. bonds, bills and coins
    C. coins   D. either coins or bills

5.____

6. Sometimes in the performance of his duties, a cashier must act alone, without advice from his superior and without reference to any books or other authority for guidance. According to this statement, a cashier must, in the exercise of his duties, sometimes display

    A. sincerity   B. caution
    C. initiative   D. courtesy

6.____

7. To say that a cashier is METICULOUS in the performance of his duties is to say that he is

    A. extremely careful   B. highly enthusiastic
    C. unusually fast   D. prone to error

7.____

8. The word NEGOTIABLE as used in business transactions means MOST NEARLY   8.____

    A. valueless   B. transferable
    C. expensive   D. profitable

9. An order which is RESCINDED is   9.____

    A. cancelled   B. adopted
    C. clarified   D. misunderstood

10. The word REMUNERATION means MOST NEARLY   10.____

    A. responsibility   B. compensation
    C. complexity   D. promotional opportunity

11. Assume that you are a cashier in an agency. Of the following, the MOST important reason why you should be courteous and tactful in dealing with visitors to your agency is that   11.____

    A. some of the visitors may show their appreciation of your courtesy by writing to your supervisor commending your work
    B. visitors who are treated courteously will probably treat you in the same manner
    C. visitors who are treated discourteously may ask your superior to take disciplinary action against you
    D. it is your responsibility to give the visitors a favorable impression of the agency

12. Assume that, as a cashier, you have been assigned the task of training a new employee in the work of collecting payments from the public.
Of the following, the MOST effective technique to follow in training this employee is for you to   12.____

    A. encourage him by praising the work he has done correctly, but do not show him the mistakes he has made
    B. insist that he obey your instructions completely even if your instructions may not be clear to him
    C. encourage him to ask questions if he does not understand any of the work
    D. give him a complete understanding of his job by showing him the incorrect, as well as the correct ways of doing his work

13. Subtract the total of 9 quarters, 17 dimes and 12 nickels from the total of 6 half-dollars, 14 quarters, 8 dimes and 6 nickels.
The *answer* is   13.____

    A. $2.05   B. $3.05   C. $3.15   D. $4.15

14. A certified check is one that   14.____

    A. states the purpose for which it is drawn
    B. has funds set aside to cover it by the bank upon which it is drawn
    C. is written by the bank upon which it is drawn
    D. requires the endorsements of both the payee and the maker before it can be cashed

15. Of the following, the MOST accurate description of a cashier's check is that it   15.____

    A. can be cashed only by the cashier of the Bank upon which it is drawn
    B. is drawn by a bank in payment for the services of one of its cashiers
    C. is drawn payable to the cashier of a bank by a depositor of the bank
    D. is drawn by a bank on its own funds and signed by its cashier

16. If, on a check, the amount payable expressed in words and the amount payable   16.____
expressed in figures are not the same, then the amount payable is the

    A. amount in figures
    B. amount in words
    C. average of the two amounts
    D. lesser of the two amounts

Questions 17 - 20.

DIRECTIONS: Column I lists four different endorsements that a man named John Doe uses to endorse checks. Column II lists the names of five types of endorsements. In questions 17 to 20, for each endorsement listed in Column I, select the correct name in Column II by which that endorsement is generally known.

    On your answer sheet, next to the number corresponding to each type of endorsement listed in Column I, write the capital letter preceding the name listed in Column II by which that endorsement is generally known.

<u>COLUMN I</u>

<u>COLUMN II</u>

17. John Doe   A. blank   17.____

18. Without recourse John Doe   B. full   18.____

19. Pay to the order of Richard Roe John Doe   C. qualified   19.____

20. Pay to the order of City Bank for deposit only John Doe   D. conditional   20.____

    E. restricted

Questions 21 - 25.

DIRECTIONS: Questions 21 to 25 are based on the following table.

COLLECTIONS BY CASHIERS FOR ONE WEEK

Name of Cashier	Monday	Tuesday	Wednesday	Thursday	Friday
Adams	$7487	$7435	$8864	$9264	$9876
Baker	9687	8643	8198	7415	8714
Taylor	7403	'6035	9722	9683	9512
Moore	6869	8212	9417	8933	9463
Foster	9129	9069	7734	8121	9596

21. Of the following, the day of the week on which the MOST money was collected is   21.____

    A. Tuesday   B. Wednesday
    C. Thursday   D. Friday

43

22. Of the following, the day of the week on which the LEAST money was collected is   22.___

    A. Monday   B. Tuesday
    C. Wednesday   D. Friday

23. The average amount collected per day by all the cashiers is   23.___

    A. less than $42,000
    B. between $42,000 and $42,500
    C. between $42,501 and $43,000
    D. more than $43,000

24. Foster's total collection for Monday, Tuesday and Friday are greater than Taylor's total   24.___
collections for the same three days by MOST NEARLY

    A. 12%   B. 17%   C. 21%   D. 83%

25. The average amount collected per cashier on Wednesday   25.___

    A. was less than the average amount collected per cashier on Monday by $328
    B. was greater than the average amount collected per cashier on Monday by $672
    C. was less than the average amount collected per cashier on Thursday by $104
    D. was greater than the average amount collected per cashier on Thursday by $886

26. A bag contains 800 coins. Of these, 10 per cent are dimes, 30 per cent are nickels, and   26.___
the rest are quarters.
The amount of money in the bag is

    A. less than $150   B. between $150 and $300
    C. between $301 and $450   D. more than $450

27. On March 1, the revenue division of a city department counted $800,000. The money   27.___
counted on March 2 was 10 per cent less than the money counted on March 1. If the
money counted on March 3 was 10 per cent greater than the money counted on March 2,
then the money counted on March 3 was

    A. $802,000   B. $792,000
    C. $720,000   D. $700,000

28. If one cashier can count a certain sum of money in 2 hours, and another cashier can   28.___
count the same sum in 3 hours, then both cashiers working together can count this sum
in

    A. 50 minutes   B. 1 hour and 10 minutes
    C. 1 hour and 12 minutes   D. 1 hour and 20 minutes

29. If the real estate tax is $4.11 per $100 of assessed valuation, the tax on real estate   29.___
assessed at $19,500 is MOST NEARLY

    A. $47   B. $650   C. $800   D. $900

30. The tax collections in a tax office for the week ending January 11th were $468,693.80. If   30.___
this amount was 20 per cent greater than the tax collections for the week ending January
4th, the tax collections for the week ending January 4th were MOST NEARLY

    A. $328,090   B. $375,000   C. $390,580   D. $393,705

31. Assume that the real estate tax rate is $4.08 per $100 of assessed valuation. If the tax on a house is $1,040.40, then the assessed valuation of the house is   31.____

   A. $25,500   B. $24,000
   C. $27,000   D. $28,500

32. Cashier X receives payments from 6 taxpayers every 15 minutes. Cashier Y receives payments from 15 taxpayers every half-hour. If Cashier X begins work at 9 a.m., and Cashier Y begins work at 9:30 a.m., the time at which the two Cashiers will have received payments from an equal number of taxpayers is   32.____

   A. 11 a.m.   B. 11:30 a.m.   C. 12 noon   D. 12:30 p.m.

33. The real estate tax on a piece of real property in a certain city is $1,082.40. If the assessed valuation of the property is $26,400, then the tax rate per $100 of assessed valuation is   33.____

   A. less than $4.05   B. between $4.05 and $4.08
   C. between $4.09 and $4.14   D. more than $4.14

34. If $300 is invested at simple interest so as to yield a return of $18 in 9 months, the amount of money that must be invested at the same rate of interest so as to yield a return of $120 in 6 months is   34.____

   A. $3000   B. $3300   C. $2000   D. $2300

35. Mr. Smith is reconciling his bank balance on November 15th by the use of the following information: 35.____
   Balance as per Bank Statement, October 31st - $15,932.20 Total Checks Outstanding, October 31st - 1,642.29 Total Deposits, November 1st to November 15th - 715.00 Total Checks Drawn, November 1st to November
   15th -   1,329.63
   According to the above information, the balance that Mr. Smith's checkbook should show as of the close of business on November 15th is MOST NEARLY

   A. $18,290   B. $16,647
   C. $13,675   D. $12,960

_____

KEY (CORRECT ANSWERS)

1.	C	11.	D	21.	D	31.	A
2.	A	12.	C	22.	B	32.	B
3.	A	13.	B	23.	C	33.	C
4.	C	14.	B	24.	C	34.	A
5.	C	15.	D	25.	B	35.	C
6.	C	16.	B	26.	A		
7.	A	17.	A	27.	B		
8.	B	18.	C	28.	C		
9.	A	19.	B	29.	C		
10.	B	20.	E	30.	C		

———

EXAMINATION SECTION
TEST 1

DIRECTIONS: Each question or incomplete statement is followed by several suggested answers or completions. Select the one that BEST answers the question or completes the statement. *PRINT THE LETTER OF THE CORRECT ANSWER IN THE SPACE AT THE RIGHT.*

1. The CHIEF purpose of a manual of *Instruction & Procedures for Money Room Employees* is to

    A. describe fully the grievance procedures available to money room employees
    B. describe methods of detecting counterfeit bills, coins, and tokens
    C. describe to money room employees the procedures that are to be used in their work
    D. help prepare money room employees to advance themselves to supervisory positions

1.____

2. The Transit, Highway, Bridge & Tunnel Authorities are created by the

    A. State Legislature   B. Public Service Commission
    C. City Council   D. Congress

2.____

3. The amount of money received and counted in the money room varies with the season of the year.
Of the following, the CHIEF reason why the money counted is not the same in each season is that there is a seasonal change in the number of

    A. cashiers   B. collecting agents
    C. passengers   D. tollroad clerks

3.____

4. The assignments of bill cage cashiers in the money room are rotated so that each cashier verifies receipts from different tollroad clerks each day.
The MOST important reason for rotating the cashiers' assignments is that

    A. the cashiers will become more familiar with various aspects of money room procedures
    B. each tollroad clerk remits a different amount of money each day
    C. collusion between cashiers and tollroad clerks is discouraged
    D. usually at least one cashier is absent every day

4.____

5. The one of the following for which a tollroad clerk would LEAST likely be held responsible is a counterfeit

    A. dollar bill   B. half-dollar
    C. nickel   D. token

5.____

6. Of the following, the MOST important precaution for a city employee to take when cashing his paycheck is to

    A. cash the check in a different bank each pay period
    B. endorse the check only when he is about to cash it
    C. insist that the check also be endorsed by the person cashing it
    D. ask the person who will cash the check to properly identify himself

6.____

7. In training a new cashier in safety procedures to be followed in the money room, it would be LEAST desirable to explain to him that

    A. the best safety device is a careful man
    B. most accidents are caused by carelessness
    C. it is more important to be careful during his training period than after he has completed his training
    D. he should always be alert to detect any possible hazards in the money room

7.__

8. The one of the following which is the SAFEST method for a cashier to use in lifting a heavy money bag is to

    A. bend his knees and back
    B. bend his knees and keep his back straight
    C. keep his knees and back straight
    D. keep his knees straight and bend his back

8.__

9. Money room procedures require that dimes, quarters, and half-dollars be bagged in amounts of $1000 each.
The CHIEF justification for this procedure is that it simplifies the

    A. problem of storage of coins
    B. assigning of work to coin cashiers
    C. counting of money for bank deposit
    D. counting of remittances from tollroad clerks

9.__

10. One of the regulations in the money room requires that after $1000 in quarters has been counted and placed in a bag, the bag must be weighed.
Of the following, the MOST important reason for weighing the bag is to

    A. eliminate the necessity for the bank to recount the money
    B. determine if an error has been made in counting the money
    C. insure against overloading the money truck carrying the money to the bank
    D. make certain that there are no counterfeit coins in the bag

10.__

Questions 11-17.

DIRECTIONS: Questions 11 through 17 are to be answered on the basis of the following information.

$100 in pennies weighs 68 pounds; $50 in nickels weighs 11 pounds; $1000 in silver of any denomination weighs 54 pounds; and 1000 tokens valued at $1.50 each weigh 3 pounds, 14 ounces.

11. The weight of $77 in pennies is MOST NEARLY _____ pounds.

    A. 52   B. 48   C. 54   D. 60

11.__

12. If the tokens in a bag weigh 1 pound, 15 ounces, then the value of these tokens is

    A. $500   B. $750   C. $50   D. $850

12.__

13. The contents of a bag containing halves, dimes, and quarters weigh 38 pounds. The amount of money in the bag is MOST NEARLY

13.____

    A. $234   B. $380   C. $760   D. $704

14. The weight of the contents of a bag containing $35 in pennies, $41 in nickels, and $730 in silver is

14.____

    A. less than 60 pounds
    B. between 60 pounds and 70 pounds
    C. between 71 pounds and 80 pounds
    D. more than 80 pounds

15. In a bag containing 1000 coins, half of the coins are nickels and the other half are dimes. The weight of the coins in the bag is MOST NEARLY _____ pounds.

15.____

    A. 8   B. 11   C. 5   D. 75

16. A bag contains $25 in pennies, $200 in quarters, $250 in dimes, and an unspecified amount in nickels.
If the weight of all the coins in the bag is 60 pounds, then the amount of money, in nickels, is

16.____

    A. less than $80   B. between $80 and $90
    C. between $91 and $100   D. more than $100

17. A bag contains $780 in nickels, dimes, and quarters.
Of the total number of coins in the bag, 10 percent are dimes, 20 percent are nickels, and the rest are quarters. If there are 400 dimes in the bag, then the weight of all the coins is

17.____

    A. less than 25 pounds
    B. between 25 pounds and 35 pounds
    C. between 36 pounds and 45 pounds
    D. more than 45 pounds

18. 27/64 expressed as a percent is

18.____

    A. 40.6250%   B. 42.1875%   C. 43.7500%   D. 45.3133%

19. $40 reduced by 3/8 of itself is

19.____

    A. $25   B. $65   C. $15   D. $55

20. $1,525.62 minus $397.29 is

20.____

    A. $1137.43   B. $1237.33   C. $1128.33   D. $1127.33

21. 12 1/2 minus 6 1/4 is

21.____

    A. 6 1/4   B. 5 3/4   C. 6 1/2   D. 5 1/2

22. 416 machine bolts $3.75 per hundred will cost

22.____

    A. $.156   B. $156.000   C. $1.560   D. $15.600

23. 21.70 divided by 1.75 equals

23.____

    A. 124.0   B. 12.4   C. 1.24   D. 0.124

24. The number 0.03125 reduced to a common fraction is   24.____

    A.   3/64   B.   1/16   C.   1/32   D.   1/13

25. 7/8 divided by 2/7 is   25.____

    A.   1/4   B.   3 1/16   C.   9/15   D.   4 1/16

26. Men's white linen handkerchiefs cost $1.29 for 3.   26.____
    The cost per dozen handkerchiefs is

    A. $7.75   B. $3.87   C. $14.48   D. $5.16

27. 357 is 6% of   27.____

    A.   2142   B.   5950   C.   4140   D.   5900

28. 572 divided by .52 is   28.____

    A.   1100   B.   110   C.   11.10   D.   11.00

29. The number of decimal places in the product of 0.4266 and 0.3333 is   29.____

    A.   8   B.   6   C.   4   D.   2

30. 72 divided by 0.009 is   30.____

    A.   0.125   B.   800   C.   8000   D.   80

31. Add 5 hrs. 13 min., 3 hrs. 49 min., and 14 min.   31.____
    The sum is _____ hrs. _____ min.

    A.   8; 16   B.   9; 16   C.   9; 76   D.   8; 6

32. The cost of 7 3/4 tons of coal at $20.16 per ton is   32.____

    A. $15.12   B. $151.20   C. $141.12   D. $156.24

33. A salesman gets a commission of 6% on his sales.   33.____
    If he wants his commission to amount to $72, he will have to sell merchandise totaling

    A. $142   B. $1200   C. $120   D. $12

34. The sum of 90.79, 79.09, 97.90, and 9.97 is   34.____

    A.   277.75   B.   278.56   C.   276.94   D.   277.93

35. John Doe borrowed $225,000.00 for 5 years at 8 1/2%.   35.____
    The annual interest charge was

    A. $15,750   B. $15,550   C. $19,125   D. $39,375

KEY (CORRECT ANSWERS)

1.	C		16.	B
2.	A		17.	D
3.	C		18.	B
4.	C		19.	A
5.	D		20.	C
6.	B		21.	A
7.	C		22.	D
8.	B		23.	B
9.	C		24.	C
10.	B		25.	B
11.	A		26.	D
12.	B		27.	B
13.	D		28.	A
14.	C		29.	A
15.	A		30.	C

31.	B
32.	D
33.	B
34.	A
35.	C

TEST 2

DIRECTIONS: Each question or incomplete statement is followed by several suggested answers or completions. Select the one that BEST answers the question or completes the statement. *PRINT THE LETTER OF THE CORRECT ANSWER IN THE SPACE AT THE RIGHT.*

1. Which number is one more than 4000?   1.___
   A. 3099   B. 3900   C. 4001   D. 3999

2. What does MCCXII mean?   2.___
   A. 712   B. 512   C. 802   D. 1212

3. What is fifty-two ten-thousandths written as a decimal?   3.___
   A. 52,010,000   B. .052   C. .0052   D. .00052

4. What is .127 expressed as a percent?   4.___
   A. 12.7%   B. 1.27%   C. 12 7/100%   D. 12 1/2%

5. What is seventy billion forty million sixty in figures?   5.___
   A. 70,400,060,000   B. 70,040,600,000
   C. 70,040,000,060   D. 70,040,000,600

6. What is the equivalent decimal of the fraction 7/8%?   6.___
   A. .875   B. .675   C. .575   D. .785

7. What is the common fraction equivalent (in its lowest terms) of .58 1/3%?   7.___
   A. 5/12   B. 174/300   C. 175/100   D. 7/12

8. The Health Department reported that 8 out of 12 children had the measles this spring.   8.___
   What fraction shows what proportion of the children had measles?
   A. 8/20   B. 2/3   C. 1/8   D. 1/12

9. The State census report showed 10,308,252 people in the State.   9.___
   How should this number be written when rounded to the nearest million?
   A. 11,000,000   B. 10,309,000
   C. 10,308,000   D. 10,000,000

10. When 3/4% of the people of Seattle have been vaccinated for smallpox, what fraction has 10.___
    been vaccinated?
    A. 3/400   B. 1/75   C. 3/4   D. 4/300

11. What percent of 33 1/3 is 8 1/3?   11.___
    A. 66 2/3%   B. 4%   C. 25%   D. 10%

12. The grades received on a clerical examination were as follows: one received a grade of 90; three received 85; four, 80; two, 75; six, 70; five, 65; two, 60; one, 55; one, 50; one, 45; one, 40; one, 30; and one, 25.
What was the average grade on the examination to the nearest tenth percent?

    A. 85.0%   B. 77.2%   C. 72.7%   D. 66.4%

12.____

13. A clerk saved 16 2/3% of his salary.
If his salary was $1800 a month, how many years and months did he work to save $13,500?

    A. 3 years, 9 months   B. 3 years, 6 months
    C. 4 years   D. 3 years, 3 months

13.____

14. Folders, each containing the same number of sheets, are filed alphabetically in a 4-drawer cabinet. The inside length of each drawer is 35 inches, and all 4 drawers are packed full. Filed under A are 43 folders occupying 7 inches.
How many folders are there in the whole cabinet?

    A. 20   B. 215   C. 860   D. 645

14.____

15. A machine operator is paid at the rate of $22.20 per hour if his hourly average production is 250 written bills. For any day in which his hourly average is below 250, his hourly rate of pay is reduced by one-sixth.
What would be his pay for a seven-hour day in which he produced 1715 written bills?

    A. $129.50   B. $136.90   C. $151.70   D. $155.40

15.____

16. A stenographer transcribes her notes at the rate of one line typed in ten seconds.
At this rate, how long (in minutes and seconds) will it take her to transcribe notes which will require seven pages of typing, 25 lines to the page?
_____ minutes, _____ seconds.

    A. 29; 10   B. 17; 50   C. 40; 10   D. 20; 30

16.____

17. During one week, a personnel agency receives 192 applications on Monday, 213 on Tuesday, 218 on Wednesday, 215 on Thursday, 102 on Friday, and 194 on Saturday.
If the agency has seven branch offices, what is the daily average number of applications received in each office for the entire week?

    A. 29   B. 27   C. 189   D. 47

17.____

18. Pencils used in an office may be bought at the price of two for 10 cents or, when bought in large quantities, at the price of $13.80 for six dozen.
What is the saving per dozen when pencils are bought at the lower rate?

    A. $.70   B. $1.00   C. $3.70   D. $7.80

18.____

19. If retirement deductions from salaries are increased from 3 1/2% to 5%, what is the monthly amount of the increase in the deduction from an $18,000 salary?

    A. $15.30   B. $52.50   C. $78.30   D. $22.50

19.____

20. A man invested $75,000 in a new business enterprise. The first year, he lost .16 2/3 of his original investment. The next year, he made a profit of 1/8 of his net worth at the beginning of that year.
His net worth at the end of the second year was what part of his original investment?

    A. 6 1/4%   B. 75%   C. 80%   D. 93 3/4%   20.____

21. 0.16 3/4 written as a percent is

    A. 16 3/4%   B. 16.3/4%   C. 0.016 3/4%   D. 0.0016 3/4%   21.____

22. $40 reduced by 3/8 of itself is

    A. $25   B. $65   C. $15   D. $55   22.____

23. $1,296.53 minus $264.87 is

    A. $1,232.76   B. $1,032.76   C. $1,031.66   D. $1,132.53   23.____

24. 12 1/2 minus 6 1/4 is

    A. 5 3/4   B. 6 1/4   C. 6 1/2   D. 5 1/2   24.____

25. A desk is marked $98, 20% 30 days, or $98, 30% 15 days cash.
If it is paid for in cash immediately on delivery, the amount paid is

    A. $66.84   B. $63.70   C. $68.40   D. $68.60   25.____

26. Add 1/4, 7/12, 3/8, 1/2, 5/6.

    A. 2 1/2   B. 2 13/24   C. 2 3/4   D. 2 15/24   26.____

27. A floor is 25 ft. wide by 36 ft. long.
To cover this floor with carpet will require _____ square yards.

    A. 100   B. 300   C. 900   D. 25   27.____

28. A salesman gets a commission of 4% on his sales.
If he wants his commission to amount to $40, he will have to sell merchandise totaling

    A. $160   B. $10   C. $1000   D. $100   28.____

29. Add 5 hours, 13 minutes; 3 hours, 49 minutes; and 14 minutes.
The sum is _____ hours, _____ minutes.

    A. 8; 16   B. 9; 16   C. 9; 76   D. 8; 6   29.____

30. John Doe borrowed $425,000 for 5 years at 9 1/2%.
The annual interest charge was

    A. $25,750   B. $35,750   C. $40,375   D. $42,950   30.____

31. 72 divided by .009 is

    A. .125   B. 800   C. 8000   D. 80   31.____

32. 345 locks at $4.15 per hundred will cost

    A. $.1432   B. $1.4320   C. $14.32   D. $143.20   32.____

54

33. The number which, when decreased by 1/5 of itself equals 132, is   33.____

    A. 165   B. 198   C. 98   D. 88

34. 285 is 5% of   34.____

    A. 1700   B. 7350   C. 1750   D. 5700

35. A store sold suits for $65 each. The suits cost $50 each.   35.____
The percentage of increase of selling price over cost is

    A. 40%   B. 33 1/2%   C. 33 1/3%   D. 30%

KEY (CORRECT ANSWERS)

1.	C	16.	A
2.	D	17.	B
3.	C	18.	A
4.	A	19.	D
5.	C	20.	D
6.	A	21.	A
7.	D	22.	A
8.	B	23.	C
9.	D	24.	B
10.	A	25.	D
11.	C	26.	B
12.	D	27.	A
13.	A	28.	C
14.	C	29.	B
15.	A	30.	C

31.	C
32.	C
33.	A
34.	D
35.	D

EXAMINATION SECTION
TEST 1

DIRECTIONS: Each question or incomplete statement is followed by several suggested answers or completions. Select the one that BEST answers the question or completes the statement. *PRINT THE LETTER OF THE CORRECT ANSWER IN THE SPACE AT THE RIGHT.*

Questions 1-10.

DIRECTIONS: Questions 1 through 10 are to be answered on the basis of the following information.

Assume you are in charge of ordering the following supplies for Unit X:

DESCRIPTION	REORDER ONLY WHEN AMOUNT FALLS TO:	AMOUNT OF EACH REORDER
Copier paper (500 pkgs/ream)	15 reams	20 reams
Copier fluid (5 bottles/carton)	2 cartons	15 cartons
Copier toner (4 bottles/pack)	1 pack	10 packs
Writing pads (12 pads/pack)	4 packs	10 packs
Typing paper (500 pkgs/ream)	3 reams	15 reams
Correction fluid (12 bottles/carton)	1 carton	5 cartons

You should assume that no supplies are reordered more than once in any one week, and that no reordering was done the first week. Reorders occur only when stated, when the facts Indicate supplies have fallen below the level required, or when the facts show logically that reordering must have occurred in order for the given totals to make sense. All reorders are filled the same day they are requested.

Other important facts:

Twenty bottles of copier fluid were used in the first week.

The amount of copier fluid at the beginning of the fourth week was double the amount of copier fluid in the unit at the beginning of the first week.

Eight bottles of copier toner were used in the first week.

Forty writing pads were used in week one, and fifty writing pads were used in week two.

The unit had twice as many cartons of correction fluid at the beginning of the first week as it had at the beginning of the third week.

In the first week, twenty-seven reams of copier paper were used.

A total of six reams of copier paper were used in the second and third weeks.

There were twelve reams of typing paper in the unit at the beginning of the third week. Now that you have the facts, here is a table to help you in answering the questions that follow. Please note that some information has already been provided. All figures in the table are in terms of reams, packs, or cartons.

	Copier paper	Copier fluid	Copier toner	Writing pads	Typing paper	Correction fluid
Beginning of week 1	42			11		
Beginning of week 2		3	2		5	
Beginning of week 3						2
Beginning of week 4						

1. How many reams of copier paper were left in the unit at the beginning of the fourth week?   1.___

    A. 9   B. 16   C. 29   D. 41

2. How many cartons of copier fluid were in the unit at the beginning of the first week?   2.___

    A. 7   B. 5   C. 23   D. 18

3. How many cartons of copier fluid were used in the unit in the second and third weeks if copier fluid was only reordered once during this time?   3.___

    A. 4
    B. 28
    C. 11
    D. Cannot be determined from the information given

4. How many packs of copier toner did the unit have at the beginning of the first week?   4.___

    A. 12   B. 4   C. 6   D. 1

5. If the unit used a total of sixteen bottles of copier toner in the second and third weeks,   5.____
   how many bottles did the unit have at the beginning of the fourth week? Assume that the
   copier fluid was only reordered once during this time.

   A. 8   B. 6   C. 24   D. 32

6. Writing pads were reordered the first time in week   6.____

   A. one   B. two   C. three   D. four

7. The number of packs of writing pads at the beginning of the fifth week was half the   7.____
   amount of the number of packs of writing pads left at the beginning of the third week.
   How many writing pads were left at the beginning of the fifth week?

   A. 6.75   B. 7   C. 81   D. 84

8. How many reams of typing paper were used by the unit in the second week?   8.____

   A. 8   B. 7   C. 12   D. 15

9. How many bottles of correction fluid did the unit use in the first and second weeks if none   9.____
   were reordered during this time?

   A. 2   B. 6   C. 12   D. 24

10. In the third week, fourteen bottles of correction fluid were used.   10.____
    This means that correction fluid was reordered

    A. the second week
    B. the third week
    C. the fourth week
    D. there was no need to reorder

KEY (CORRECT ANSWERS)

1.	C		6.	B
2.	A		7.	C
3.	A		8.	A
4.	B		9.	D
5.	D		10.	B

EXAMINATION SECTION
TEST 1

DIRECTIONS: Each question or incomplete statement is followed by several suggested answers or completions. Select the one that BEST answers the question or completes the statement. *PRINT THE LETTER OF THE CORRECT ANSWER IN THE SPACE AT THE RIGHT.*

1. The stock items on the purchase order should be the same as those on the shipment receipt at time of delivery.
   In general, it is BEST to check this at the time that the stock items are

   A. received in the storehouse
   B. ordered by the agency using the material
   C. issued by the storehouse personnel
   D. certified for payment

   1._____

2. Sawdust and shredded paper are materials that are generally used in which one of the following operations?

   A. Packing   B. Inventory
   C. Spraying   D. Transporting

   2._____

3. Storage areas with good air circulation and ventilation are generally considered

   A. *good,* only in hot and humid weather
   B. *good,* to retard mold growth
   C. *poor,* due to danger of fire
   D. *poor,* because of cleaning costs

   3._____

4. To get the best use from storage areas, it is usually BEST to use high ceilinged areas for storing

   A. heavy, bulky stock items
   B. lightweight stock items
   C. loose stock items in small bins
   D. extremely large-sized stock items

   4._____

5. The section of the storeroom that can carry the least weight should generally NOT be used for storing stock items that

   A. have a large size   B. have a small size
   C. are very heavy   D. are very light

   5._____

6. Where should you store unusually large and heavy stock items that are used very often?

   A. As close to the shipping and receiving areas as possible
   B. Away from work areas, such as shipping and receiving
   C. On hand trucks until the using agency asks for the item
   D. Only in storage areas which are outside the storehouse

   6._____

7. Which of the following would be MOST important in deciding how wide the space should be between cartons stacked in a storage area?

   7._____

A. Type of equipment that will be used to handle the stock
B. Size of the storage area
C. Number of employees in the storage area
D. How far the storage area is away from the receiving area

8. Stock items that might break, chip, or be crushed should be packed   8.___

A. *tightly* with items touching each other
B. *loosely* in a heavy wood container
C. *tightly* with little movement allowed between items
D. *tightly* with cushioning material between items

9. Suppose that some stock items delivered by truck are found to be damaged before they   9.___
are unloaded.
Which of the following actions would be BEST to take?

A. Take the damaged stock and then give it out first to prevent further damage
B. Refuse to take any damaged items
C. Tell the driver of the truck to return the entire shipment
D. Tell your supervisor about the damage so that he can take the necessary steps

10. It is dangerous to store gasoline because   10.___

A. it can only be stored in specially constructed rooms in a storehouse
B. it gives off vapors that can easily burn
C. it can explode when moved around
D. no one has found a safe way of storing gasoline

11. Gases are usually stored under pressure in steel cans. Which of the following is the   11.___
LEAST dangerous practice?

A. Allowing the cans to come in contact with electrical circuits
B. Lifting the cans by their valves
C. Allowing the cans to touch each other
D. Keeping the valves on the cans open after the gas has been used up

12. Acids are a danger in storage because leakage may result in a sudden fire if contact is   12.___
made with other chemicals. When storing acids, the one of the following practices which
is INCORRECT is to

A. keep them in heavy duty metal cans
B. store them in isolated areas
C. protect the containers against breakage
D. keep flames or lit matches out of areas where acids are stored

13. Tape with a cellophane backing will become wrinkled and lumpy if stored in an area that   13.___
is

A. warm   B. cool   C. damp   D. very dry

14. To keep wooden furniture from warping and twisting, it should be stored in an area that is   14.___

A. warm and dry   B. warm and damp
C. cool and dry   D. cool and damp

15. Which one of the following items should NOT be stored in a very dry storage area?   15.____

    A. Soup cubes   B. Baking soda
    C. Tea leaves   D. Lettuce

16. Some food items can easily spoil.   16.____
    If they are packed in torn sacks or broken boxes, they should be stored

    A. in exactly the same way as other items
    B. just after fixing the sacks or boxes
    C. inside a bin in the storage area
    D. after spraying with DDT or another insect spray

17. Of the following items, which one is MOST likely to be damaged by insects?   17.____

    A. Iron pipes   B. Rubber inner tubes
    C. Plastic tubing   D. Grain products

18. Which one of the following items, when stored properly, has the SHORTEST storage life?   18.____

    A. Baked products   B. Noodles
    C. Cornstarch   D. Rolled oats

19. Which one of the following food items is LEAST likely to give off smells in a storehouse?   19.____

    A. Cheese   B. Onions
    C. Fresh peaches   D. Baking powder

20. The word *inventory* means the practice of counting all the stock items within each class   20.____
    of items.
    However, before an inventory can be done,

    A. the stock items must be thoroughly cleaned
    B. all stock items must be located and identified
    C. old stock items should be thrown away
    D. stock items that have been returned by the user should not be counted

----

KEY (CORRECT ANSWERS)

1.	A	11.	C
2.	A	12.	A
3.	B	13.	C
4.	B	14.	C
5.	C	15.	D
6.	A	16.	B
7.	A	17.	D
8.	D	18.	A
9.	D	19.	D
10.	B	20.	B

TEST 2

DIRECTIONS: Each question or incomplete statement is followed by several suggested answers or completions. Select the one that BEST answers the question or completes the statement. *PRINT THE LETTER OF THE CORRECT ANSWER IN THE SPACE AT THE RIGHT.*

1. *Pliers* may BEST be classified under   1._

    A. food products   B. tools
    C. office supplies   D. machinery

2. *White pine lumber* may BEST be classified under   2._

    A. building materials   B. laboratory materials
    C. safety materials   D. seeds and plants

3. *Linseed oil* may BEST be classified under   3._

    A. drugs and chemicals   B. painters' supplies
    C. building materials   D. fuel and fuel oils

4. *Ceiling tiles* may BEST be classified under   4._

    A. office supplies   B. hardware
    C. electrical supplies   D. building materials

5. *Floor finish remover* may BEST be classified under   5._

    A. insecticides   B. drugs
    C. machinery   D. cleaning supplies

6. *Arm slings* may BEST be classified under   6._

    A. hospital supplies   B. clothing
    C. school supplies   D. office supplies

7. *Staplers* may BEST be classified under   7._

    A. office supplies   B. laboratory supplies
    C. machinery and metals   D. engineering supplies

8. *Canvas stretcher* may BEST be classified under   8._

    A. laboratory apparatus   B. hospital supplies
    C. clothing   D. tools

9. *Switches* may BEST be classified under   9._

    A. camera supplies   B. vehicles
    C. electrical supplies   D. pipes and pipe fittings

10. *Bandages* may BEST be classified under   10._

    A. laboratory equipment   B. surgical instruments
    C. hospital supplies   D. hose and belting

Questions 11-15.

DIRECTIONS: Questions 11 through 15 are to be answered on the basis of the information given below.

LISTING OF PAPER
FOUND IN STOCKROOM A, ON APRIL 30

	Quantity Ordered by Stockroom A (in dozen reams)	Quantity in Stock Before Delivery (in dozen reams)	Cost Per Ream	Location of Stock in Stockroom	
8 1/2"x11" Blue	17	5	$0.94	Bin	A7
8 1/2"x11" Buff	8	3	$0.93	Bin	A7
8 1/2"x11" Green	11	4	$0.95	Bin	B4
8 1/2"x11" Pink	10	4	$0.93	Bin	B4
8 1/2"x11" White	80	15	$0.86	Bin	A8
8 1/2"x13" White	76	12	$1.02	Bin	A8
8 1/2"x14" Blue	7	2	$1.19	Bin	A7
8 1/2"x14" Buff	7	3	$1.18	Bin	A7
8 1/2"x14" Green	5	2	$1.20	Bin	B4
8 1/2"x14" Pink	8	4	$1.18	Bin	B4
8 1/2"x14" White	110	28	$1.15	Bin	A8
8 1/2"x14" Yellow	2	1	$1.23	Bin	C6

11. How many reams of 8 1/2"x13" paper will there be in stock if only one-half of the amount ordered is delivered? _____ reams.   11.____

   A. 456   B. 600   C. 912   D. 1056

12. Suppose all ordered material is delivered.   12.____
     The bin that will have the MOST reams of paper is

   A. A7   B. A8   C. B4   D. C6

13. Suppose all ordered material has been delivered.   13.____
     What is the approximate value of all 8 1/2"x11" paper which is in Bin B4?

   A. $27   B. $171   C. $198   D. $327

14. How many reams of white paper of all sizes were ordered? _____ reams.   14.____

   A. 55   B. 266   C. 660   D. 3192

15. Before any of the orders were delivered, the following requests were filled and removed   15.____
     from the stockroom:
     2 dozen reams 8 1/2"x11" Blue; 2 dozen reams 8 1/2"x11" Green;
     7 dozen reams 8 1/2"x11" White; 5 dozen reams 8 1/2"x13" White;
     1 dozen reams 8 1/2"x14" Green; 13 dozen reams 8 1/2"x14" White.
     How many reams of paper were left in the stockroom after the above requests were filled?

   A. 30   B. 53   C. 636   D. 996

Questions 16-20.

DIRECTIONS: Questions 16 through 20 are to be answered SOLELY on the basis of the information given in the table below.

CONTROLLED DRUG A

Time Period	Purchase Order Number	Quantity Ordered	*Quantity Delivered by Vendor	Quantity Distributed during 2-week Period	Inventory Balance end of 2-Week Period
April 23-May 6	110,327	105 ounces	135 ounces	27 ounces	108 ounces
May 7-May 20	111,437	42 ounces	40 ounces	39 ounces	109 ounces
May 21-June 3	112,347	37 ounces	27 ounces	32 ounces	104 ounces
June 4-June 17	112,473	35 ounces	35 ounces	45 ounces	94 ounces
June 18-July 1	114,029	40 ounces	40 ounces	37 ounces	97 ounces

*Delivery is made on first day of time period.

16. The *difference* between Quantity Ordered and Quantity Delivered was greatest on Purchase Order Number   16.__

    A. 110,327   B. 111,437   C. 112,347   D. 112,473

17. The *difference* between the total number of ounces ordered and the total number of ounces delivered on April 23 through June 18 is _____ ounces.   17.__

    A. 17   B. 18   C. 19   D. 20

18. Suppose that average weekly usage was expected to be 26 ounces per week. Your supervisor has asked you to tell him whenever inventory balances get below a four-week level.   18.__
    Under these conditions, you should have told your supervisor during the two-week period beginning

    A. April 23, May 21, June 4, June 18
    B. May 21, June 4, June 18
    C. May 21, June 18
    D. June 4, June 18

19. The GREATEST decreases in inventory balances happened between the two-week periods beginning   19.__

    A. April 23 and May 7   B. May 7 and May 21
    C. May 21 and June 4   D. June 4 and June 18

20. Suppose a new program has been started at your hospital and the weekly usage of Drug   20._____
A is expected to be 52 ounces per week.
If your supervisor must keep on hand a four-week supply, then the amount that should
be delivered for the two-week period beginning on July 2 is _____ ounces.

   A. 52   B. 111   C. 208   D. 211

_____

KEY (CORRECT ANSWERS)

1.	B	11.	B
2.	A	12.	B
3.	B	13.	D
4.	D	14.	D
5.	D	15.	C
6.	A	16.	A
7.	A	17.	B
8.	B	18.	D
9.	C	19.	C
10.	C	20.	B

_____

TEST 3

DIRECTIONS: Each question or incomplete statement is followed by several suggested answers or completions. Select the one that BEST answers the question or completes the statement. *PRINT THE LETTER OF THE CORRECT ANSWER IN THE SPACE AT THE RIGHT.*

1. Suppose that 3-foot high boxes are to be stacked in one pile on a 4-inch platform. In addition, 4-inch thick separators are placed between each layer of boxes. Suppose that the ceiling is 22 feet high, and there must be at least 1 1/2 feet of space between the ceiling and the stacked boxes.
What is the GREATEST number of boxes that can be stacked?

   A. 4   B. 5   C. 6   D. 7   1.__

2. A part of a storeroom measures 14 1/2 feet by 6 1/4 feet.
The number of square feet in this part is _____ square feet.

   A. 8 1/4   B. 20 3/4   C. 90 5/8   D. 94 3/4   2.__

3. How many *cubic* feet of storage space would be taken up by 20 boxes, when each box measures 2 feet high, 2 feet wide, and 3 feet long? _____ cubic feet.

   A. 12   B. 27   C. 140   D. 240   3.__

4. Suppose that a truckload of canned items has been unloaded. There are six rows of boxes with seven boxes in each row. Each box has two dozen cans in it.
How many cans are there all together?

   A. 24   B. 144   C. 510   D. 1008   4.__

5. Suppose that the average weekly use of tissue amounts to 180 rolls.
At least how many boxes must be ordered for a 4-week period if there are 144 rolls in each box?

   A. 2   B. 3   C. 4   D. 5   5.__

6. Suppose that a stockroom started the week with an initial supply of 3 gross of pencils and that one gross equals 144 pencils. After orders were filled, the stockroom had an inventory at the end of the week as follows: 2 gross of 4H pencils; 3 dozen 2B pencils; 1 1/2 dozen HB pencils; and 15H pencils.
How many pencils were ordered?
_____ pencils.

   A. 22   B. 45   C. 75   D. 97   6.__

7. How many 18-inch pieces can be cut from 10 lengths of 8-foot glass tubing?
_____ pieces.

   A. 47   B. 50   C. 53   D. 56   7.__

8. Suppose a roll of wire is 27 feet 3 inches long. A piece of wire measuring 18 feet 9 inches in length is cut from the roll.
What is the length of wire left on the roll? _____ feet _____ inches.

   A. 7; 3   B. 7; 6   C. 8; 3   D. 8; 6   8.__

9. Suppose that 25% of a delivery of canned peaches was spoiled.   9.____
   If 36 cans were spoiled, then the delivery had a total of _____ cans.

   A. 9   B. 25   C. 144   D. 180

10. Suppose that a one-quart can of white flat ceiling paint weighs 5 pounds.   10.____
    What is the GREATEST number of quart cans that can be stored on a shelf that sup-
    ports 167 pounds?
    _____ quart cans.

    A. 5   B. 33   C. 41   D. 67

11. Assume that the following orders were filled from a 55-gallon drum of oil: 9 pints, 7 pints,   11.____
    2 quarts, 6 quarts, 3 gallons.
    How much oil is left in the drum?
    _____ gallons.

    A. 0   B. 8   C. 45   D. 48

12. Suppose a certain chemical can be given out only in one kilogram containers. 2.2   12.____
    pounds equals 1 kilogram.
    The GREATEST number of kilograms that can be obtained from 100 pounds of this
    chemical is MOST NEARLY

    A. 41   B. 43   C. 45   D. 47

13. A truckload of supplies weighing 1 1/2 tons is unloaded by 5 workers in 2 hours. Suppose   13.____
    that the work is equally divided among the workers.
    How many pounds of supplies can be unloaded by each worker per hour?
    _____ pounds per hour.

    A. 150   B. 300   C. 450   D. 600

14. A room is 40 yards long and 15 yards wide. One square foot of floor can support 100   14.____
    pounds.
    What is the GREATEST weight that can be supported by the floor in that room?

    A. 600   B. 5,400   C. 60,000   D. 540,000

15. Suppose that an empty storage area can be safely loaded with 324,000 lbs. of stock   15.____
    items.
    How many boxes can be stored in this area if each box has in it one dozen cans that
    weigh 3 pounds each?

    A. 8,500   B. 9,000   C. 9,500   D. 10,000

16. 18 boxes of oranges with 1000 oranges in each box are in a storehouse.   16.____
    How many orders of 1,440 oranges each can be filled completely?

    A. 10   B. 11   C. 12   D. 13

17. Suppose that the following 3 deliveries of dry cereal are made each day: 30 cartons with   17.____
    60 boxes in each carton, 25 cartons with 60 boxes in each carton, and 20 cartons with
    100 boxes in each carton.
    If daily orders total 400 boxes, how many more boxes must be delivered in order to
    have enough boxes for a 14-day supply?

A. 50   B. 100   C. 200   D. 300

18. Suppose that 11 pints of distilled water are used each day in the hospital laboratories   18.___
    and that a pint costs 7 cents.
    What would a 30-day supply of distilled water cost?
    About

    A. $23   B. $24   C. $25   D. $27

19. If 2000 lbs. of salt costs $500, what does one pound cost?   19.___

    A. $.20   B. $.22   C. $.25   D. $.27

20. The price of floor wax is 15 cents a quart. On orders of over 100 gallons, however, 2.5%   20.___
    is subtracted from the price of every quart in the order.
    What is the cost of 200 gallons of floor wax?

    A. $115   B. $117   C. $119   D. $121

———————

KEY (CORRECT ANSWERS)

1.	C	11.	D
2.	C	12.	C
3.	D	13.	B
4.	D	14.	D
5.	D	15.	B
6.	C	16.	C
7.	B	17.	D
8.	D	18.	A
9.	C	19.	C
10.	B	20.	B

———————

TEST 4

DIRECTIONS: Each question or incomplete statement is followed by several suggested answers or completions. Select the one that BEST answers the question or completes the statement. *PRINT THE LETTER OF THE CORRECT ANSWER IN THE SPACE AT THE RIGHT.*

1. Employees who must lift and carry stock items should be careful to avoid injury. When an employee lifts or carries stock items, which of the following is the LEAST safe practice?

    A. Keep the legs straight and lift with the back muscles
    B. Keep the load as close to the body as possible
    C. Get a good grip on the object to be carried
    D. First determine if the item can be lifted and carried safely

1.____

2. For warning and protection, the color red is usually used for

    A. indicating high temperature stockroom areas
    B. floor markings
    C. location of first aid supplies
    D. stop buttons, lights for barricades, and other dangerous locations

2.____

3. Reporting rattles, squeaks, or other noises in equipment to your maintenance supervisor is

    A. *bad;* too much attention to squeaks like these keep important safety problems from being noticed
    B. *bad;* each person should oil and care for his own equipment
    C. *good;* these sounds may mean that the equipment should be fixed
    D. *good;* it shows the supervisor that you are a good worker

3.____

4. If you often get cuts on your hands from handling different kinds of cartons and boxes, the BEST thing for you to do is

    A. keep from handling those kinds of cartons and boxes
    B. ask that better boxes and cartons be used
    C. toughen up your hands
    D. wear protective gloves

4.____

5. A low, movable platform used for stacking material in a warehouse is called a *pallet*. When lifting and moving *pallets* with a forklift, how should a stockman place the forks?

    A. As wide apart as possible
    B. As close together as possible
    C. Close together and tilted forward
    D. Wide apart and tilted forward

5.____

Questions 6-11.

DIRECTIONS: Questions 6 through 11 are to be answered ONLY on the information given in the following table.

RECORD OF INCOMING FREIGHT SHIPMENTS

Received	Purchase Order No.	Amount		Shipper	No. of Items	Weight	Shippers' Catalog No.
		Prepaid	To Be Collected				
1/7	9616	$15.10		Harding Grove Equip	14	170	28
1/12	3388		$ 2.00	People's Paper Inc.	10	50	091
1/12	8333		$106.19	Falls Office Supply	25	2500	701
2/2	7126		$ 9.00	Leigh Foods	175	4000	47
2/13	4964		$ 3.09	McBride Paper Co.	14	75	83
4/13	3380	$14.09		Central Hardware	14	1750	019
4/30	7261		$ 6.90	Northwestern Foods	121	2100	13
5/12	9166	$10.50		Harding Grove Equip.	15	50	36
5/17	6949		$ 4.19	Black's Paper Co.	40	65	743
5/31	6691		$ 20.00	Central Hardware	16	600	563
6/30	5388	$ 9.75		Harding Grove Equip.	15	15	420
6/30	8308		$ 22.50	Falls Office Supply	19	290	97
8/23	8553		$ 4.90	Tremont Paper Inc.	75	570	36
9/12	5338	$ 6.91		Northeast Hardware	51	901	071
10/15	6196	$12.00		Mobray Hardware	60	786	131

6. All items listed in the above table were delivered by   6.___

    A. U.S. mail   B. freight
    C. air express   D. ship

7. On what date was the LARGEST number of items received?   7.___

    A. 2/2   B. 2/13   C. 4/30   D. 5/17

8. If all items shipped by Falls Office Supply on 1/12 were of equal weight, how much did   8.___
    each item weigh? _____ pounds.

    A. 10   B. 25   C. 100   D. 250

9. If the names of the shippers were put in alphabetical order, which of the following should be put after McBride Paper Company?   9.____

   A. Northeast Hardware   B. Leigh Foods
   C. Northwestern Foods   D. Mobray Hardware

10. What is the purchase order number for the Harding Grove Equipment shipment that was received on 5/12?   10.____

   A. 9166   B. 5388   C. 9616   D. 6691

11. All items that cost less than five dollars ($5.00) came from shippers of   11.____

   A. paper   B. foods
   C. hardware   D. office supplies

Questions 12-16.

DIRECTIONS: Questions 12 through 16 are to be answered SOLELY on the basis of the information contained in the following passage.

Floors in warehouses, storerooms, and shipping rooms must be strong enough to stay level under heavy loads. Unevenness of floors may cause boxes of materials to topple and fall. Safe floor load capacities and maximum heights to which boxes may be stacked should be posted conspicuously so all can notice it. Where material in boxes, containers, or cartons of the same weight is regularly stored, it is good practice to paint a horizontal line on the wall indicating the maximum height to which the material may be piled. A qualified expert should determine floor load capacity from the building plans, the age, and condition of the floor supports, the type of floor, and other related information.

Working aisles are those from which material is placed into and removed from storage. Working aisles are of two types: transportation aisles, running the length of the building, and cross aisles, running across the width of the building. Deciding on the number, width, and location of working aisles is important. While aisles are necessary and determine boundaries of storage areas, they reduce the space actually used for storage.

12. According to the passage above, how should safe floor load capacities be made known to employees?   12.____
They should be

   A. given out to each employee
   B. given to supervisors only
   C. printed in large red letters
   D. posted so that they are easily seen

13. According to the passage above, floor load capacities should be determined by   13.____

   A. warehouse supervisors   B. the fire department
   C. qualified experts   D. machine operators

14. According to the above passage, transportation aisles   14.____

   A. run the length of the building
   B. run across the width of the building

C. are wider than cross aisles
D. are shorter than cross aisles

15. According to the passage above, working aisles tend to 15.___

    A. take away space that could be used for storage
    B. add to space that could be used for storage
    C. slow down incoming stock
    D. speed up outgoing stock

16. According to the passage above, unevenness of floors may cause 16.___

    A. overall warehouse deterioration
    B. piles of stock to fall
    C. materials to spoil
    D. many worker injuries

Questions 17-20.

DIRECTIONS: Questions 17 through 20 are to be answered SOLELY on the basis of the information contained in the following passage.

Planning for the unloading of incoming trucks is not easy since generally little or no advance notice of truck arrivals is received. The height of the floor of truck bodies and loading platforms sometimes are different; this makes necessary the use of special unloading methods. When available, hydraulic ramps compensate for the differences in platform and truck floor levels. When hydraulic ramps are not available, forklift equipment can sometimes be used, if the truck springs are strong enough to support such equipment. In a situation like this, the unloading operation does not differ much from unloading a railroad boxcar. In the cases where the forklift truck or a hydraulic pallet jack cannot be used inside the truck, a pallet dolly should be placed inside the truck, so that the empty pallet can be loaded close to the truck contents and rolled easily to the truck door and platform.

17. According to the passage above, unloading trucks is 17.___

    A. easy to plan since the time of arrival is usually known beforehand
    B. the same as loading a railroad boxcar
    C. hard to plan since trucks arrive without notice
    D. a very normal thing to do

18. According to the above passage, which materials handling equipment can make up for 18.___
the difference in platform and truck floor levels?

    A. Hydraulic jacks   B. Hydraulic ramps
    C. Forklift trucks   D. Conveyors

19. According to the above passage, what materials handling equipment can be used when 19.___
a truck cannot support the weight of forklift equipment?

    A. A pallet dolly   B. A hydraulic ramp
    C. Bridge plates   D. A warehouse tractor

20. Which is the BEST title for the above passage?   20.____
    A. Unloading Railroad Boxcars
    B. Unloading Motor Trucks
    C. Loading Rail Boxcars
    D. Loading Motor Trucks

KEY (CORRECT ANSWERS)

1.	B	11.	A
2.	D	12.	D
3.	C	13.	C
4.	D	14.	A
5.	A	15.	A
6.	B	16.	B
7.	A	17.	C
8.	C	18.	B
9.	D	19.	A
10.	A	20.	B

SAMPLE QUESTIONS

BIOGRAPHICAL INVENTORY

The questions included in the Biographical Inventory ask for information about you and your background. These kinds of questions are often asked during an oral interview. For years, employers have been using interviews to relate personal history, preferences, and attitudes to job success. This Biographical Inventory attempts to do the same and includes questions which have been shown to be related to job success. It has been found that successful employees tend to select some answers more often than other answers, while less successful employees tend to select different answers. The questions in the Biographical Inventory do not have a single correct answer. Every choice is given some credit. More credit is given for answers selected more often by successful employees.

These Biographical Inventory questions are presented for illustrative purposes only. The answers have not been linked to the answers of successful employees; therefore, we cannot designate any "correct" answer(s).

DIRECTIONS: You may only mark ONE response to each question. It is possible that none of the answers applies well to you. However, one of the answers will surely be true (or less inaccurate) for you than others. In such a case, mark that answer. Answer each question honestly. The credit that is assigned to each response on the actual test is based upon how successful employees described themselves when honestly responding to the questions. *PRINT THE LETTER OF THE CORRECT ANSWER IN THE SPACE AT THE RIGHT.*

1. Generally, in your work assignments, would you prefer   1._____
    A. to work on one thing at a time
    B. to work on a couple of things at a time
    C. to work on many things at the same time

2. In the course of a week, which of the following gives you the GREATEST   2._____
    satisfaction?
    A. Being told you have done a good job.
    B. Helping other people to solve their problems.
    C. Coming up with a new or unique way to handle a situation.
    D. Having free time to devote to personal interests.

―――――――

EXAMINATION SECTION

TEST 1

DIRECTIONS: Each question or incomplete statement is followed by several suggested answers or completions. Select the one that BEST answers the question or completes the statement. *PRINT THE LETTER OF THE CORRECT ANSWER IN THE SPACE AT THE RIGHT.*

1. While a senior in high school, I was absent
    A. never
    B. seldom
    C. frequently
    D. more than 10 days
    E. only when I felt bored

1._____

2. While in high school, I failed classes
    A. never
    B. once
    C. twice
    D. more than twice
    E. at least four times

2._____

3. During class discussions in my high school classes, I usually
    A. listened without participating
    B. participated as much as possible
    C. listened until I had something to add to the discussion
    D. disagreed with others simply for the sake of argument
    E. laughed at stupid ideas

3._____

4. My high school grade point average (on a 4.0 scale) was
    A. 2.0 or lower
    B. 2.1 to 2.5
    C. 2.6 to 3.0
    D. 3.1 to 3.5
    E. 3.6 to 4.0

4._____

5. As a high school student, I completed my assignments
    A. as close to the due date as I could manage
    B. whenever the teacher gave me an extension
    C. frequently
    D. on time
    E. when they were interesting

5._____

6. While in high school, I participated in
    A. athletic and non-athletic extracurricular activities
    B. athletic extracurricular activities
    C. non-athletic extracurricular activities
    D. no extracurricular activities
    E. mandatory afterschool programs

6._____

7. In high school, I made the honor roll   7._____
   - A. several times
   - B. once
   - C. more than once
   - D. twice
   - E. I cannot remember

8. Upon graduation from high school, I received _____ honors.   8._____
   - A. academic and non-academic
   - B. academic
   - C. non-academic
   - D. no
   - E. I cannot remember

9. While attending high school, I worked at a paid job or as a volunteer   9._____
   - A. never
   - B. every so often
   - C. 5 to 10 hours a month
   - D. more than 10 hours a month
   - E. more than 15 hours a month

10. During my senior year of high school, I skipped school   10._____
   - A. whenever I could
   - B. once a week
   - C. several times a week
   - D. not at all
   - E. when I got bored

11. I was suspended from high school   11._____
   - A. not at all
   - B. once or twice
   - C. once or twice, for fighting
   - D. several times
   - E. more times than I can remember

12. During high school, my fellow students and teachers considered me   12._____
   - A. above average
   - B. below average
   - C. average
   - D. underachieving
   - E. underachieving and prone to fighting

13. An effective leader is someone who   13._____
   - A. inspires confidence in his/her followers
   - B. inspires fear in his/her followers
   - C. tells subordinates exactly what they should do
   - D. creates an environment in which subordinates feel insecure about their job security and performance
   - E. makes as few decisions as possible

14. While a student, I spent my summers and holiday breaks   14._____
    A. in summer or remedial classes
    B. traveling
    C. working
    D. relaxing
    E. spending time with my friends

15. As a high school student, I cut classes   15._____
    A. frequently
    B. when I didn't like them
    C. sometimes
    D. rarely
    E. when I needed the sleep

16. In high school, I received academic honors   16._____
    A. not at all
    B. once
    C. twice
    D. several times
    E. I cannot remember

17. As a student, I failed _____ classes.   17._____
    A. no
    B. two
    C. three
    D. four
    E. more than four

18. Friends describe me as   18._____
    A. introverted
    B. hot-tempered
    C. unpredictable
    D. quiet
    E. easygoing

19. During my high school classes, I preferred to   19._____
    A. remain silent during discussions
    B. do other homework during discussions
    C. participate frequently in discussions
    D. argue with others as much as possible
    E. laugh at the stupid opinions of others

20. As a high school student, I was placed on academic probation   20._____
    A. not at all
    B. once
    C. twice
    D. three times
    E. more than three times

21. At work, being a team player means to   21._____
   - A. compromise your ideals and beliefs
   - B. compensate for the incompetence of others
   - C. count on others to compensate for your inexperience
   - D. cooperate with others to get a project finished
   - E. rely on others to get the job done

22. My friends from school remember me primarily as a(n)   22._____
   - A. person who loved to party
   - B. ambitious student
   - C. athlete
   - D. joker
   - E. fighter

23. My school experience is memorable primarily because of   23._____
   - A. the friends I made
   - B. the sorority/fraternity I was able to join
   - C. the social activities I participated in
   - D. my academic achievements
   - E. the money I spent

24. A friend who is applying for a job asks you to help him pass the   24._____
    mandatory drug test by substituting your urine sample for his. You should
   - A. help him by supplying the sample
   - B. supply the sample and insist he seek drug counseling
   - C. supply the sample, but tell him that this is the only time you'll help
     in this way
   - D. call the police
   - E. refuse

25. As a student, I handed in my assignments when   25._____
   - A. they were due
   - B. I could get an extension
   - C. they were interesting
   - D. my friends reminded me to
   - E. I was able to

KEY (CORRECT ANSWERS)

1. A	11. A	21. D
2. A	12. A	22. B
3. C	13. A	23. D
4. E	14. C	24. E
5. D	15. D	25. A
6. A	16. D	
7. A	17. A	
8. A	18. E	
9. E	19. C	
10. D	20. A	

TEST 2

DIRECTIONS: Each question or incomplete statement is followed by several suggested answers or completions. Select the one that BEST answers the question or completes the statement. *PRINT THE LETTER OF THE CORRECT ANSWER IN THE SPACE AT THE RIGHT.*

1. At work you are accused of a minor infraction which you did not commit. Your first reaction is to
    A. call a lawyer
    B. speak to your supervisor about the mistake
    C. call the police
    D. yell at the person who did commit the infraction
    E. accept the consequences regardless of your guilt or innocence

1._____

2. As a student, I began to prepare for final exams
    A. the night before taking them
    B. when the professor handed out the review sheets
    C. several weeks before taking them
    D. when my friends began to prepare for their exams
    E. the morning of the exam

2._____

3. At work, I am known as
    A. popular
    B. quiet
    C. intense
    D. easygoing
    E. dedicated

3._____

4. The most important quality in a coworker is
    A. friendliness
    B. cleanliness
    C. good sense of humor
    D. dependability
    E. good listening skills

4._____

5. In the past year, I have stayed home from work
    A. frequently
    B. only when I felt depressed
    C. rarely
    D. only when I felt overwhelmed
    E. only to run important errands

5._____

6. For me, the best thing about school was the
    A. chance to strengthen my friendships and develop new ones
    B. chance to test my abilities and develop new ones
    C. number of extracurricular activities and clubs
    D. chance to socialize
    E. chance to try several different majors

6._____

7. As an employee, my weakest skill is   7._____
    A. controlling my temper
    B. organizational ability
    C. ability to effectively understand directions
    D. ability to effectively manage others
    E. ability to communicate my thoughts in writing

8. As an employee, my greatest strength would be   8._____
    A. my sense of loyalty
    B. organizational ability
    C. punctuality
    D. dedication
    E. ability to intimidate others

9. If asked by my company to learn a new job-related skill, my reaction   9._____
would be to
    A. ask for a raise
    B. ask for overtime pay
    C. question the necessity of the skill
    D. cooperate with some reluctance
    E. cooperate with enthusiasm

10. When I disagree with others, I tend to   10._____
    A. listen quietly despite my disagreement
    B. laugh openly at the person I disagree with
    C. ask the person to explain their views before I respond
    D. leave the conversation before my anger gets the best of me
    E. point out exactly why the person is wrong

11. When I find myself in a situation which is confusing or unclear, my   11._____
reaction is to
    A. pretend I am not confused
    B. remain calm and, if necessary, ask someone else for clarification
    C. grow frustrated and angry
    D. walk away from the situation
    E. immediately insist that someone explain things to me

12. If you were placed in a supervisory position, which of the following   12._____
abilities would you consider to be most important to your job
performance?
    A. Stubbornness
    B. The ability to hear all sides of a story before making a decision
    C. Kindness
    D. The ability to make and stick to a decision
    E. Patience

13. What is your highest level of education?   13._____
    A. Less than a high school diploma
    B. High school diploma or equivalency
    C. Graduate of community college
    D. Graduate of a four-year accredited college
    E. Degree from graduate school

14. When asked to supervise other workers, your approach should be to   14._____
    A. ask for management wages since you're doing management work
    B. give the workers direction and supervise every aspect of the process
    C. give the workers direction and then allow them to do the job
    D. hand the workers their job specifications
    E. do the work yourself, since you're uncomfortable supervising others

15. Which of the following best describes you?   15._____
    A. Need little or no supervision
    B. Resent too much supervision
    C. Require as much supervision as my peers
    D. Require slightly more supervision than my peers
    E. Require close supervision

16. You accept a job which requires an ability to perform several tasks at once. What is the best way to handle such a position?   16._____
    A. With strong organizational skills and close attention to detail
    B. By delegating the work to someone with strong organizational skills
    C. Staying focused on one task at a time, no matter what happens
    D. Working on one task at a time until each task is successfully completed
    E. Asking your supervisor to help you

17. Which of the following best describes your behavior when you disagree with someone? You   17._____
    A. state your own point of view as quickly and loudly as you can
    B. listen quietly and keep your opinions to yourself
    C. listen to the other person's perspective and then carefully point out all the flaws in their logic
    D. list all of the ignorant people who agree with the opposing point of view
    E. listen to the other person's perspective and then explain your own perspective

18. As a new employee, you make several mistakes during your first week of work. You react by   18._____
    A. learning from your mistakes and moving on
    B. resigning
    C. blaming it on your supervisor
    D. refusing to talk about it
    E. blaming yourself

19. My ability to communicate effectively with others is   19._____
    A. below average
    B. average
    C. above average
    D. far above average
    E. far below average

20. In which of the following areas are you most highly skilled?   20._____
   A. Written communication
   B. Oral communication
   C. Ability to think quickly in difficult situations
   D. Ability to work with a broad diversity of people and personalities
   E. Organizational skills

21. As a worker, you are assigned to work with a partner whom you dislike.   21._____
   You should
   A. immediately report the problem to your supervisor
   B. ask your partner not to speak to you during working hours
   C. tell your colleagues about your differences
   D. tell your partner why you dislike him/her
   E. work with your partner regardless of your personal feelings

22. During high school, what was your most common afterschool activity?   22._____
   A. Remaining after school to participate in various clubs and
      organizations (band, sports, etc.)
   B. Making up for missed classes
   C. Punishment or detention
   D. Going straight to an afterschool job
   E. Spending the afternoon at home or with friends

23. During high school, in which of the following subjects did you receive the   23._____
   highest grades?
   A. English, history, social studies
   B. Math, science
   C. Vocational classes
   D. My grades were consistent in all subjects
   E. Classes I liked

24. When faced with an overwhelming number of duties at work, your   24._____
   reaction is to
   A. do all of the work yourself, no matter what the cost
   B. delegate some responsibilities to capable colleagues
   C. immediately ask your supervisor for help
   D. put off as much work as possible until you can get to it
   E. take some time off to relax and clear your mind

25. Which of the following best describes your desk at your current or most   25._____
   recent job?
   A. Messy and disorganized
   B. Neat and organized
   C. Messy but organized
   D. Neat but disorganized
   E. Messy

KEY (CORRECT ANSWERS)

1. B	11. B	21. E
2. C	12. D	22. A
3. E	13. E	23. D
4. D	14. C	24. B
5. C	15. A	25. B
6. B	16. A	
7. E	17. E	
8. D	18. A	
9. E	19. C	
10. C	20. C	

TEST 3

DIRECTIONS: Each question or incomplete statement is followed by several suggested answers or completions. Select the one that BEST answers the question or completes the statement. *PRINT THE LETTER OF THE CORRECT ANSWER IN THE SPACE AT THE RIGHT.*

1. When asked to take on extra responsibility at work, in order to help out a coworker who is overwhelmed, your response is to
    A. ask for overtime pay
    B. complain to your supervisor that you are being taken advantage of
    C. help the coworker to the best of your ability
    D. ask the coworker to come back some other time
    E. give the coworker some advice on how to get his/her job done

1._____

2. At my last job, I was promoted
    A. not at all
    B. once
    C. twice
    D. three times
    E. more than three times

2._____

3. You are faced with an overwhelming deadline at work. Your reaction is to
    A. procrastinate until the last minute
    B. procrastinate until someone notices that you need some help
    C. notify your supervisor that you cannot complete the work on your own
    D. work in silence without asking any questions
    E. arrange your schedule so that you can get the work done before the deadline

3._____

4. When you feel yourself under deadline pressure at work, your response is
    A. make sure you keep to a schedule which allows you to complete the work on time
    B. wait until just before the deadline to complete the work
    C. ask someone else to do the work
    D. grow so obsessive about the work that your coworkers feel compelled to help you
    E. ask your supervisor immediately for help

4._____

5. Which of the following best describes your appearance at your current or most recent position?
    A. Well-groomed, neat and clean
    B. Unkempt, but dressed neatly
    C. Messy and dirty clothing
    D. Unshaven and untidy
    E. Clean-shaven, but sloppily dressed

5._____

6. Which of the following best describes the way you react to making a difficult decision?

    A. Consult with the people you're closest to before making the decision

    B. Make the decision entirely on your own

    C. Consult only with those people whom your decision will affect

    D. Consult with everyone you know, in an effort to make a decision that will please everyone

    E. Forget about the decision until you have to make it

6._____

7. If placed in a supervisory role, which of the following characteristics would you rely on most heavily when dealing with the employees you supervise?

    A. Kindness

    B. Cheeriness

    C. Honesty

    D. Hostility

    E. Aloofness

7._____

8. When confronted with gossip at work, your typical reaction is to

    A. participate

    B. listen without participating

    C. notify your supervisor

    D. excuse yourself from the discussion

    E. confront your coworkers about their problem

8._____

9. In the past two years, how many jobs have you held?

    A. None

    B. One

    C. Two

    D. Three

    E. More than three

9._____

10. In your current or most recent job, your favorite part of the job is the part which involves

    A. telling other people what they're doing wrong

    B. supervising others

    C. working without supervision to finish a project

    D. written communication

    E. oral communication

10._____

11. Your supervisor asks you about a colleague who is applying for a position which you also want. You react by

    A. commenting honestly on the colleague's work performance

    B. enhancing the person's negative traits

    C. informing your supervisor about your colleague's personal problems

    D. telling your supervisor that you would be better in the position

    E. refusing to comment

11._____

12. Which of these best describes your responsibilities in your last job?   12._____
    A. Entirely supervisory
    B. Much supervisory responsibility
    C. Equal amounts of supervisory and non-supervisory responsibility
    D. Some supervisory responsibilities
    E. No supervisory responsibilities

13. How much written communication did your previous or most recent job   13._____
require of you?
    A. A great deal
    B. Some
    C. I don't remember
    D. A small amount
    E. None

14. In the past two years, how many times have you been fired from a job?   14._____
    A. None
    B. Once
    C. Twice
    D. Three times
    E. More than three times

15. How many hours per week have you spent working for volunteer   15._____
organizations in the past year?
    A. 10 to 20
    B. 5 to 10
    C. 3 to 5
    D. 1 to 3
    E. None

16. Your efforts at volunteer work usually revolve around which of the   16._____
following types of organizations?
    A. Religious
    B. Community-based organization working to improve the community
    C. Charity on behalf of the poor
    D. Charity on behalf of the infirm or handicapped
    E. Other

17. Which of the following best describes your professional history?   17._____
Promoted at _____ coworkers.
    A. a much faster rate than
    B. a slightly faster rate than
    C. the same rate as
    D. a slightly slower rate than
    E. a much slower rate than

18. Which of the following qualities do you most appreciate in a coworker?   18._____
    A. Friendliness
    B. Dependability
    C. Good looks
    D. Silence
    E. Forgiveness

19. When you disagree with a supervisor's instructions or opinion about how to complete a project, your reaction is to
    A. inform your supervisor that you refuse to complete the project according to his or her instructions
    B. inform your colleagues of your supervisor's incompetence
    C. accept your supervisor's instructions in silence
    D. voice your concerns and then complete the project according to your own instincts
    E. voice your concerns and then complete the project according to your supervisor's instructions

19._____

20. Which of the following best describes your reaction to close supervision and specific direction from your supervisors? You
    A. listen carefully to the direction, then figure out a way to do the job more effectively
    B. complete the job according to the given specifications
    C. show some initiative by doing the job your way
    D. ask someone else to do the job for you
    E. listen carefully to the directions, and then figure out a better way to do the job which will save more money

20._____

21. At work, you are faced with a difficult decision. You react by
    A. seeking advice from your colleagues
    B. following your own path regardless of the consequences
    C. asking your supervisor what you should do
    D. keeping the difficulties to yourself
    E. working for a solution which will please everyone

21._____

22. If asked to work with a person whom you dislike, your response would be
    A. to ask your supervisor to allow you to work with someone else
    B. to ask your coworker to transfer to another department or project
    C. talk to your coworker about the proper way to behave at work
    D. pretend the coworker is your best friend for the sake of your job
    E. set aside your personal differences in order to complete the job

22._____

23. As a supervisor, which of the following incentives would you use to motivate your employees?
    A. Fear of losing their jobs
    B. Fear of their supervisors
    C. Allowing employees to provide their input on a number of policies
    D. Encouraging employees to file secret reports regarding colleagues' transgressions
    E. All of the above

23._____

24. A fellow worker, with whom you enjoy a close friendship, has a substance   24._____
abuse problem which has gone undetected. You suspect the problem
may be affecting his job. You would
     A. ask the worker if the problem is affecting his job performance
     B. warn the worker that he must seek counseling or you will report
        him
     C. wait a few weeks to see whether the worker's problem really is
        affecting his job
     D. discuss it with your supervisor
     E. wait for the supervisor to discover the problem

25. In the past two months, you have missed work   25._____
     A. never
     B. once
     C. twice
     D. three times
     E. more than three times

KEY (CORRECT ANSWERS)

1. C	11. A	21. A
2. C	12. D	22. E
3. E	13. B	23. C
4. A	14. A	24. D
5. A	15. C	25. A
6. A	16. B	
7. C	17. A	
8. D	18. B	
9. B	19. E	
10. C	20. B	

Made in the USA
Las Vegas, NV
09 April 2024

88383441R00070